Los Gobernadores y Los Franciscanos

de Nuevo Mexico:1598-1700

The Governors and Franciscans

of **New Mexico**: 1598-1700

HARRY FULSOM

iUniverse LLC
Bloomington

Los Gobernadores y Los Franciscanos de Nuevo Mexico:1598-1700
The Governors and Franciscans of New Mexico: 1598-1700

iUniverse books may be ordered through booksellers or by contacting:

iUniverse LLC
1663 Liberty Drive
Bloomington, IN 47403
www.iuniverse.com
1-800-Authors (1-800-288-4677)

Because of the dynamic nature of the Internet, any web addresses or links contained in this book may have changed since publication and may no longer be valid. The views expressed in this work are solely those of the author and do not necessarily reflect the views of the publisher, and the publisher hereby disclaims any responsibility for them.

Any people depicted in stock imagery provided by Thinkstock are models, and such images are being used for illustrative purposes only.
Certain stock imagery © Thinkstock.

ISBN: 978-1-4620-0881-0 (sc)
ISBN: 978-1-4620-0882-7 (e)

Printed in the United States of America

iUniverse rev. date: 02/24/2014

CONTENTS

PREFACE

I would like to present a study of the relations which took place between the Governors and the Franciscans of New Mexico during the 1600's from actual as well as potential human standpoints. As the essential causes—intolerance, use and abuse of the Pueblo Indians—of the Pueblo Revolt of 1680 often contain the effects—human recognition (Governor Bernardo Lopez de Mendizabal (1659-61), human reconciliation (Governor Juan Francisco Treviño (1675-77), the eventual disappearance of the encomienda (trusteeship) and el repartimiento (requisition for forced labor) from Pueblo Indian life.

THE GOVERNORS OF NEW MEXICO: 1598-1704

Don Juan de Oñate 1598-1607

Cristóbal de Oñate 1608-10

Don Pedro de Peralta 1610-14

Don Bernardino de Ceballos 1614-18

Don Juan de Eulate 1618-25

Don Felipe Sotelo y Osario 1625-29

Don Francisco de Silva Nieto 1629-32

Don Francisco Mora y Ceballos 1632-35

Don Francisco Martínez de Baeza 1635-37

Don Luís de Rosas 1637-41

Don Juan Sierra y Valdéz 1641

Don Alonso Pacheco y Heredía 1642-44

Don Fernando de Arguello y Carvajal 1644-47

Don Luís Guzman y Figueroa 1647-49

Don Hernando de Ugarte y Concha 1649-53

Don Juan Sarmiento y Xaca 1653-56

Don Juan Manso de Contreras 1656-59

Don Bernardo de López de Mendízabal 1659-61

Don Diego de Peñalosa 1661-64

Don Juan de Miranda 1664-65

Don Fernando de Villanueva 1665-68

Don Medrano de Mesia 1668-71

Don Juan de Miranda 1671-75

Don Juan Francisco Treviño 1675-77

Don Antonio de Otermín 1677-83

Don Domingo de Cruzate 1683-86

Don Pedro Reneros de Posada 1686-89

Don Domingo de Cruzate 1689-91

Don Diego de Vargas 1691-97

Don Pedro Rodríquez y Cubero 1697-1703

Courtesy of Lansing Bloom for the New Mexico Historical Review

CHAPTER I

THE FOUNDATION OF SANTA FE

The motives for the behavior which characterized the everyday relations between the governors and the Franciscans of New Mexico during the seventeenth century do not always appear clear and comprehensive. The actual responses of the governors to the Franciscans and the responses of the Franciscans to the governors provide us with a blueprint for those Spaniards numerous of whom came to develop their own settlement principles and mind sets across New Mexico. The results of the behavior which took place between the governors, the Franciscans, Peninsulares (Spaniards born on the Iberían Península, Criollos (individuals born in Nueva España and/or Mexico), mestizos (individuals born of one Anglo individual and one Indian individual), the Apaches of New Mexico, the Apaches of the Great Plains, certain Indians of the Southwest and the Pueblo Indians of New Mexico, offer us certain insights into various political, religious and cultural histories of seventeenth century New Mexico.

With the entry of the Spaniards into New Mexico, the peninsular, criollo, mestizo, Pueblos, Apache and Comanche ethnic groups met and intermingled, transcending the idea of the Spanish creation of the Republic of the Spaniards and the Republic of the Indians.

Aside from certain Indians natural to the Tlaxcala Valley of Mexico (future settlers of the Analco [lands on the other side of the river] districts of Santa Fe), all of whom entered New Mexico with the Francisco Vázquez de Coronado expedition of 1540-43, soldier, alcalde ordinario [magistrate], Juan Martínez Montoya, Spanish settlers and Spanish Franciscans may have been, between 1607 and 1610, among the first Spaniards to select (for safety and ecological motives) a narrow valley surrounded on the northeast by Las Sangre de Cristo

1

Montañas and on the northwest by Valley of el Río Grande, as the future site of Santa Fe.[1] Pedro de Peralta, the official founder of Santa Fe, whose contracts dates from March 30, 1609, was as the third governor of New Mexico, the first governor of New Mexico to refuse to temper relations between the governors and Franciscans in New Mexico during the 1600's. The Peralta expedition was formed of nineteen soldiers, nine to eleven Franciscans, 13 carts, 150 oxen, 500 cattle as well as Mexican men and women.

The Franciscan and fourth commissary of New Mexico, after the Franciscan Friars, Alonso Martínez, Juan de Escalona (Escalona had served with reservation under Governor Oñate) and Francisco Escobar, all whom of had served under Governor Juan de Oñate, Alonso Peinado, who was among the first persons to confront the attitude of the supposed first agent of the Mexican Inquisition, the Franciscan Friar, Isidro Ordoñëz, set a precedent between 1610 and 1612, cooperating with Governor Peralta, which was not to take place again in New Mexico until the reign of Governor Francisco Silva Nieto (1629-32). [2]

Between 1493 and 1810, the Spaniards' accumulation and transference of their mineral wealth, such as gold and silver, from the New World to the Old World, and their agricultural wealth, such as sugar cane plants (1493) and banana plants (1516), from the Old to the New World and their participation in European wars provided sufficient motives for Dutch, English and French interventions across and apart from the Spanish Empire in the New World.[3] On the other hand, the monetary caution shown by Philip II (1556-98), who created the Colonization Laws of 1573 to amend the motives for the entries of the Spaniards into the New World and temper the entry of Spanish miners and slavers into New Mexico, with New Mexico in mind, would contribute greatly, (without his being aware of it) to the general political destabilization of Spanish institutions in the Spanish Vice-Royalty of Nueva España and eventually, the province of New Mexico as well. Santa Fe was constructed between 1610-20, according to Pueblo Indian labor; even though Governor Peralta had to admit that he did not have often provisions sufficient for the constructors of Santa Fe.[4]

---

[1]   Thomas Chávez, Sustainable Santa Fe. {Santa Fe, New Mexico. 2008. Page 24

[2]   Franz Scholes. Problems of the Early Ecclesiastical History of New Mexico. The New Mexico Historical Review. Volume VII. Pages 32-66

[3]   Burkholder, Marc. Johnson, Lyman. Spanish Colonization of Latin America. {London, England. Oxford Press. 1989

[4]   Twitchell, Ralph. Antigua Santa Fe. The University of New Mexico Press. 1997

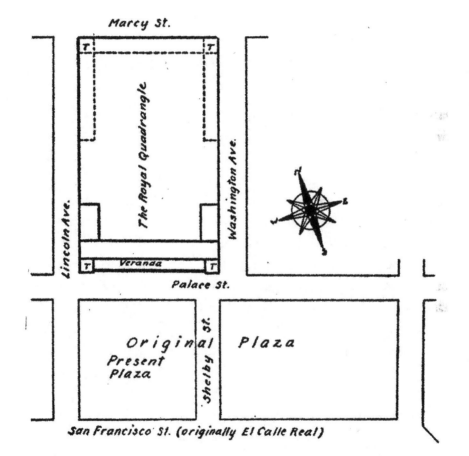

Marcy St.

Lincoln Ave.

The Royal Quadrangle

Washington Ave.

T T

T Veranda T

Palace St.

Original
Present
Plaza

Shelby St.

Plaza

San Francisco St. (originally El Calle Real)

CHAPTER II

THE SPANIARDS' PRINCIPAL FOUNDATION LAWS OF THE **1600's**

Spanish conquistadors, such as Francisco Vázquez de Coronado (1540-43) and Juan de Oñate (1598-07), each of whom came to New Mexico during the sixteenth century, were dependent in order to rule, on the Requirement of 1512, which had been drawn up under the Regency of the Spanish Queen, Juana de Castilla and the reign of the Spanish King, Fernando de Aragón. The Requirement of 1512 {first of three Spanish secular decrees of the sixteeenth century to have a decided effect on the relations of the Spaniards} [Consider Governor Oñate's conquest, conversion and possession speech given at Santo Domingo or Kewa Pueblo Pueblo on July 7th, 1598] with los indios e indias of the New World required such Indians to participate in Spanish religious rights, swear allegiance to the pope and to the Spanish king.

> But if you do not do this and wickedly and intentionally delay to do so I certify to you that, with help of God, we shall forcibly enter into your country and make war against you in all ways that we can, and shall subject you to the yoke and obedience of the church and their highnesses. We shall take your goods as our highnesses and shall do harm and damage that we can, as to vassals who do not obey and refuse to receive their lord and resist and contradict him; and we protest that the deaths that shall accrue from this are your fault, and not those who come with us. And as we

have said this to make this requirement, we request that the notaries here present that they should be witnesses of this requirement.[5]

Had Queen Isabella (1451-1504), the person most responsible for the discovery of the New World, been living at the time, the Requirement of 1512, may not have come into existence. "For she had advised, in letters, the Franciscans to regard the Indians of the New World."

The New Laws of the Indies, which the Spanish King, Carlos I, drew up in 1542 (due in part to the influence of the Dominican priest, Bartolomé de las Casas)[6] liberated in principle in not in fact the Indians of the New World from la encomienda; prevented in principle if not in fact the overwork of the Indians of the New World; made the Indians vassals (subjects) of the Spanish king; made proper treatment of the Indians a prerequisite for their bondage; and requested (largely ineffectively for a time) that Spaniards' Peruvian and Mexican encomienda grants revert, after the passage of two generations, and equally ineffectively in New Mexico [at last until 1640], to the Spanish king.

The Colonization Laws of 1573 or the Ordinances of his Majesty for the Discovery, Conquest and Pacification which had been drawn up under the rule of Philip II came into existence due largely to the incapacity of the expeditions of the Franciscan Friar Marcos de Niza and Francisco Vázquez de Coronado to treat with the Indians of the New Land to the North. The Ordinances were to make a largely successful effort to prohibit Spanish miners and slavers from entering New Mexico.

As subjects of el repartimiento (the Spanish Institution for the acquisition of individual and communal labor), numerous Pueblo Indians were forced to work during and beyond their working day for the Spaniards.[7]

To maintain in bondage the Indians of the New World, the Spaniards introduced the encomienda grant. La encomienda was ideally a form of social, economic and military trusteeship. Under la encomienda, the Indians of New Mexico were forced to provide, food, blankets, and service in defense of the Spanish frontier and, in Mexico, money to the Spaniards in exchange for human protection and religious instruction.

---

[5] Quoted in lecture by Linder, Peter. Latin American Studies. Highlands University. Las Vegas, New Mexico. 2002.

[6] Burkholder, Marc. Johnson, Lyman. The Spanish Colonization of Latin America. {London, England. Oxford Press. 1989} Page 69

[7] Ibid. Page 36

In New Mexico, the service roles would be, in part, reversed. The soldier-settlers or settler—soldiers (after the departure from San Gabriel of two-thirds of the Oñate expedition for the mining site of Santa Barbara, Nueva Vizcaya, in October of 1601),[8] and encomenderos [possessors of encomienda grants for the lands of the Pueblo Indians and Moqui-Hopi of northern Arizona] had always to serve as protectors of the Santa Fe and the Santa Fe provision carts; from Santa Fe to Paso del Norte {El Paso} and from Paso del Norte to Santa Fe. The encomenderos had to promise to live in Santa Fe; even though their encomiendas were to be discoverable among houses and pueblos of the Pueblo and Moqui Indians.

The Pueblo Indians of New Mexico were forced for a time to pay tribute to the Catholic Church, Spanish governor, the Spanish viceroy and the Spanish king. Even though the law position of Corregidor or corrector was known to have come to Santa Fe, the division of the monetary recompense known as the Royal Fifth among the Spaniards may not have been fully adhered to in Santa Fe. Under la encomienda, the Puebloans were forced to provide (twice a year for a time) one manta or cotton blanket (six human hands in width) and one fanega or 1.5 bushels of corn to the Spanish settlers and often deer and buffalo hides, depending on the location of the Spanish encomienda grant [Taos and Pecos were especially rich sites for the application of the Spaniards' encomienda grant] to the Spanish encomenderos whose limit (down from hundreds) was set, for motives of efficiency, by el virrey Escalona, at thirty-five during the 1640's.

Second in command of the Spanish Empire (the Council of the Indies apart) only to the Spanish kings, during the 1600's, Spanish Viceroys [el virrey Lorenzo Suárez de Mendoza took it upon himself to the authorize the entry of the Rodríquez-Chamuscado expedition of June 5-6th, 1581 to New Mexico], such as the Count of Monterrey (1586-1590); the Marquess of Monteclaros (1603-1607); Luís Velasco II (1590-95 1607-1610) and García Guerra)1611-12) did not define the respective jurisdictions of the governors and the Franciscans in New Mexico.

---

[8]   Kessell, John. Kiva, Cross and Crown. Department of the Interior, Washington D. C. 1979.

CHAPTER **III**

THE GOVERNORS AND FRANCISCANS OF NEW MEXICO

In the Spring of 1607, the new commissary of provisions and supposed first agent of the Mexican Inquisition in New Mexico, Ysidro Ordoñez and Fraile Lázaro Ximnenes had returned to Mexico with examples of gold and silver and the claim that as many as eight thousand Pueblo Indians had been converted to Catholicism, neutralizing, in time, the decision of Philip III, would set out upon to abandon New Mexico in 1608.[9]

As commissary and first agent of the Mexican Inquisition, he would set out to establish his if not the place of the Franciscans vis a vis Governor Peralta. With one eye on the previous Keresan uprising against the Spaniards in Acoma (pronounced Akema) Pueblo, Governor Peralta sent, with the desire of quelling a possible pueblo revolt in 1613, a detachment of soldiers north in order to collect the annual Spring en lieu of Fall tribute from Taos Pueblo. Upon hearing of Governor Peralta's intent and encountering his tribute contingent in Nambé, comisario Ordöñez ordered the soldiers in question to return to Santa Fe in order to attend the Feast of the Pentecost {originally an Old Testament Feast Day before evolving into the day in which the Holy Spirit descended on the disciples of Jesus}, which had been scheduled for July 26, 1613.

Upon discovering his tribute contingent in attendance at the Feast of the Pentecost, within the convent of Santa Fe, which was located across the plaza from the site of the governor's residence, Peralta was stung with disbelief. He ordered them to set forth once again for Taos Pueblo. Upon observing Peralta's exercise of secular authority in the convent

---

[9]   Hallenbeck, Cleve. Land of the Conquistadores. Caxton Press. Caldwell, Idaho. 1950.

of Santa Fe, Ordóñez ordered the caretaker of Santa Fe, Luís Tirado, to place a notification of the excommunication of Governor Peralta on the door of the convent of Santa Fe. The male and female citizens of Santa Fe numerous of whom had sided with the governor and local soldiers during the Peralta-Ordóñez controversies had been and would continue to be forced to sit through the Sunday tirades of Ordóñez, which were, according to one Franciscan, not for the women of Santa Fe to hear.

During late June and early July of 1613, Peralta wrote to the New Mexican Franciscan Andrés Perguerra, in order to demand tribute labor from the Pueblo of San Lázaro for the renewal of construction on Santa Fe. Upon hearing of Peralta's demand, Ordóñez requested that the tribute labor in question be taken from the far pueblos of las Salinas of the Estancia Basin or the pueblos of the Southern Piro within the Southern Rio Grande sub-region.

In response to Governor Peralta's demand for tribute labor for the renewal of construction on Santa Fe, Luís Tirado, the guardian of the convent of Santa Fe, removed the governors' chair from inside and threw it outside the convent onto the Santa Fe Plaza on a certain Holy Day of Obligation.

Peralta, as a result of having been excommunicated once again in Santa Fe, consequently made an effort to ride to Mexico City, in order to present his side of the Ordóñez, Peralta controversy to el virrey Diego de Cordova. Governor Peralta, along with his lieutenant, Juan de Escharramado, was detained (for approximately a year) by comisario Ordóñez and the members of his faction (select Franciscans only) on the night of August 12, 1613 in the Pueblo Ysleta and incarcerated in the Pueblo of Sandia.

The Royal Quadrangle, Santa Fe, 1610   *Chris Weber 1913*

For New Mexico to flourish, however, new agreements would have to come into being between the Spaniards of New Mexico and the Pueblos of New Mexico.

With idea of reconciling for a time the differences between state and religious authority in New Mexico, Bernardino de Ceballos (1614-18) was appointed by el virrey Diego de Cordova to be the fourth governor of New Mexico in 1614. As a former Admiral in the Spanish Navy, Ceballos cooperated with comisario Ordóñez long enough for him to despoil Pedro Peralta of his possessions before sending him down el Camino Real to face el virrey and two members of la Audiencia. Ceballos, who had befriended, Juan de Escharramado, a friend of Pedro de Peralta, was left to face the caretaker of the Santa Fe convent, Luís Tirado, who excommunicated the former as much being an un-believer as for being a friend of Juan de Escharramado.

At the conclusion of reign of Ysidro Ordóñez in 1616, the Holy Office had sixteen friars in New Mexico. With the arrival of seven Franciscans on the commissary carts of either late 1616 or early 1617, the number of Franciscans whom had come to New Mexico reached twenty-three. The Franciscans would have personnel and vistas or visiting sites in the Tewa Pueblos of Santo Domingo, Nambé and San Ildefenso; the Keresan Pueblo of Zia; the Tano Pueblos of San Lázaro and Galisteo; the Southern Tiwa Pueblos of Sandia and Ysleta; and the Tompiro Pueblo of Chilili.

CHAPTER IV

THE ROYAL ORDER OF 1620

During January of 1621, the Spanish King, Philip III, who felt appalled by the treatment the Franciscans of New Mexico had dealt out to his appointees, governors Pedro de Peralta (1610-1614) and Bernardino de Ceballos (1614-1618), issued with the compliance of el virrey, Diego de Cordova, el marqués de Guadalcázar, "The Royal Order of 1620;" in order to make a rational, distant, belated, one sided, and, hence, un-successful effort to regulate the jurisdiction of the Franciscans vis a vis the governors of New Mexico.[10]

"Don Felipe, by the grace of God, King of Castile, of Leon, of the two Sicilies, of Jerusalem, of Portugal, of Navarre, of Granada, of Cordova, of Corsica, of Murcia, of Jaen, of the Algarbes, of Algeciras, of Gibraltar, of the Canary Islands, of the Islands and mainland of the oceanic sea (Atlantic); archduke of Austria, Duke of Burgundy, Brabant, and Milan—to you the venerable padre, Fray Estéban Perea of the seraphic order to San Francisco, custodio of the religious of the said order who reside in the province of New Mexico; know ye, that in the Council which el Marqués de Guadalcázar, my cousin, viceroy, governor and capitán-general of Nueva España, and president of my Royal Audiencia, and chancery who resides in this city of Mexico on the 29th of July of this year with the 3 señor oidores or judges of my said Audiencia, with the attendance of my fiscal in accordance with the royal order which I have given; there were seen certain letters, missives, memorials depositions from those said provinces to my said Viceroy, by various persons, ecclesiastic as well

---

[10] Lansing Bloom. The Royal Order of 1620. The New Mexico Historical Review. July 1930. Page 288

as lay, through which account has been given of the strifes over jurisdiction which there have been and are, between you and the said Custodian and my governor; you, the said Father, claiming that, by virtues of the bulls of his Holiness, Leo X and Adrian VI, you have in those province authority and jurisdiction supreme as well as ordinary ad universatatem causaram so you can take cognizance of any ecclesiastical matters whatever, and can issue any censure and interdict any person of whatever state, condition and preeminence they may be, imposing upon them punishments at your command and claiming further that they, my said governor should not and could not decree or determine any matter touching his said government without first consulting you."

In all due fairness, the next virrey of Nueva España, el marqués de Cerralvo, would write to the Santa Fe community imploring its members neither to cut the hair of the Pueblo Indians nor interfere in Pueblo elections.[11]

On the other hand, the New Mexico governors' imposition of secular authority in the domain of the Franciscans; use of Pueblo Indian labor; extraction of tribute; acquisition of the material goods of former governors and imposition of trade among the Indians of the Great Plains and the Southwest, determined the relations which would develop between the governors, the Franciscans, the soldier-settlers, the Apaches of the Great Plains and New Mexico and the Pueblo Indians of New Mexico

The first Franciscans of New Mexico,(not all of whom would depart, prior to the departure of the expedition in question for New Mexico, from the Oñate expedition for one motive or another] may have been the only persons of the era in Nueva España to consider themselves apart from the jurisdiction of either the Viceroy of Nueva España or the governors of New Mexico. The Franciscans developed their own Ytenerario: "requesting that el virrey Gaspar Zuniga y Acevedo, the Count of Monterrey (1585-90), increase the number of Franciscans going to New Mexico from six to ten; prohibit the governors from interfering in the construction of Franciscan churches and schools; guarantee the Natives freedom from coercion in order not to incite them to aggressive actions; reserve the right of the Franciscans to communicate with the Viceroy and his superiors; permit the Franciscans unlimited entry into Indian country; appoint an Indian woman as translator for the expedition and transfer

---

[11]   Lansing Bloom. The Royal Order of 1620. The New Mexico Historical Review. July 1930. Page 288

young Spaniards to the New Land to the North.[12] Although el virrey would not honor the request of the Franciscans, it would set the tone for the relations which were to develop between the Franciscans and the Governors of New Mexico during the 1600's w in New Mexico.

The settler-soldiers' acquisition of often the best lands nearest to the lands of the Pueblo Indians and lands of the Franciscans led to a series of controversies between the soldier-settlers and the Franciscans over the use of the land and the Pueblo Indians.

The New Mexico encomenderos' application of la encomienda lawfully and un-lawfully to the Pueblo Indians of New Mexico, determined to a degree, the relations, which would develop between the encomenderos, the governors, the Franciscans, and common settlers and the Pueblo Indians of New Mexico.

---

[12]   Simmons, Marc. The Last Conquistador. University of Oklahoma Press. Norman, Oklahoma. 1991.

CHAPTER **V**

FRANCISCAN RULE IN NEW MEXICO

I
n order to counter-balance, perhaps, the in-capacity of Pedro de Peralta to temper the orders of Isidro Ordóñez, el marqués de Guadalcázar had chosen, almost to confront and most certainly to frustrate, for a time, the Franciscans' effort to convert the Pueblo Indians to Catholicism, a Spanish soldier, Juan de Eulate, (1618-25), to be the fifth governor of New Mexico.

According to the renown New Mexico historian, France Scholes, "Eulate was petulant, without tact and irreverent, a soldier whose actions were marked by disdain for the Catholic Church." Without a doubt, Eulate promoted the conservation of the idols or "human effigies" of the Pueblos and polygamy (marriage of one man with more than one woman) among the Pueblos of New Mexico not only to taunt the Franciscans, but to receive as much tribute as possible from the Pueblos of New Mexico. Although Eulate promoted, against even the protests of the Franciscans, the enslavement of the actual and so-called orphans of the pueblos within the houses of Santa Fe, he condemned the use of men and oxen for the construction of the Pecos Church, stating in no un-certain terms to two would be constructors of it, "I would like you to walk out to Pecos and, then, return to Santa Fe with yokes and straps of oxen on our backs."[13]

With designation of Miguel de Chavarría as the new custos of New Mexico in 1621, (appointed in 1620) and due to his previous friendship with Governor Eulate, construction commenced on the second Franciscan church to have been constructed at Pecos Pueblo.[14]

---

[13]   Kessell, John. Kiva, Cross and Crown. Department of the Interior, Washington D. C. 1979.

[14]   Kesssell, John. Kiva, Cross and Crown. {Washington D. C. Department of the Interior. 1979.} Page 120

The voice of the new virrey Rodrigo Pacheco Osorio, el marqués de Cerralvo, which reigned in Mexico City, would only echo in New Mexico. Nonetheless, he ordered the governors and the Franciscans neither to interfere in Pueblo elections nor cut the hair of the Pueblo Indians.

As an advocate of Pueblo Indian labor and of the belief that Pueblo Indian overseers should organize Pueblo Indian labor, Eulate, who selected Pueblo Indians to clear land on the edge of Santa Fe for the construction of his hacienda, may have been the first Spaniard to breed livestock in New Mexico not only for the acquisition of wealth, but for the transference of such wealth to Mexico.[15]

If the reign of Bernardino de Ceballos had been an involuntary witness to the arrival of seven Franciscans, and the creation of New Mexico as a Custody (prior to May, 17, 1620) of the Chapter of Saint Paul)[16] with its own Custodian or custos Estéban Perea [1616-17-1621] and Miguel de Chavarría, in 1621, the seven year reign of Governor Eulate, which would be characterized by the suppression and subsequent renewal of construction on the convents or los conventos, visiting stations or vistas and churches or Iglesias of New Mexico, would usher in seven years of Franciscan dominance across New Mexico if not future Arizona (1625-1632).

In order for the Indians of Pecos to serve as human beings in the socio-economic world of New Mexico, Andrés Juárez, custodian of Pecos Pueblo, arranged for Alonso de Oñate, the brother of Juan de Oñate, to send carpenters, along with their axes, chisels and plains to Pecos Pueblo. If nothing came easy for the Pueblo Indians of New Mexico during the seventeenth century, native artisan development within Spanish clerical workshops was to create in iron, wood and leather, a socio-economic craftsperson whose works the Spaniards and Pueblos would one day draw on.[17]

Having been constructed of adobe bricks—nine and one half inches in width by eighteen inches in length by three inches in height (each brick weighed about forty-two pounds) and roof beams or vigas of forty-four feet in length over its entrance and twenty-seven and one half feet over its apse—by female and male members of Pecos and Santa Fe, the Pecos church with its forty-four buttresses or contras-fuertes and its two friars quarters, which were located on its second floor, was according to John Kessell not to endure very much like the

[15]   Jones, O. Pueblo Warriors. The University of Oklahoma Press. 1966.
[16]   France Scholes. Early Ecclesiastical History. New Mexico Historical Review. 1932. V. 7. Pages 32-73
[17]   Kessell, John. Kiva, Cross and Crown. {Washington D. C Department of the Interior. 1979. } Page. 124.

relationships which may have developed between the caciques or chiefs, the Pueblo governors and the Portuguese and Spanish governors of New Mexico. Apart from and not because of Governor Eulate, Andrés Juárez saw the construction of his church take place between 1625 and 1626.

According to the New Mexico historian, France Scholes, the sixth governor of New Mexico, Felipe de Sotelo Osorio (1625-29), was profane, blasphemous and lacking in respect for the clergy and the Mass, immoral and suspect in faith. Without a doubt, Sotelo-Osorio not only gambled with the soldier-settlers of Santa Fe but was known to have pulled out a short-sword during arguments with the soldier-settlers of Santa Fe. The Franciscans upbraided Sotelo-Osorio for acting like a heretic or non-believer during Mass, demanding that everyone rise on his entry into the domain of the Franciscans. In order to challenge the ecclesiastical privilege and perpetual immunity offered to the Spanish community by the Franciscans of New Mexico, Sotelo-Osorio ordered the arrest of a mulatto who suspected of rustling cattle had taken refuge in the convent of Santa Fe; even if he were holding on to the crucifix. In order to contribute in-directly to the ideal of cultural integration in New Mexico, Sotelo Osorio had taken a "converted" Pueblo woman as his mistress; an act not un-common among Spaniards of the era in New Mexico.

The Franciscan, Alonso de Benavides (1626-29), was an ethnologist (student of cultural practices) and man of promotion as well. Benavides, who participated in the construction of ten churches in New Mexico, saw the world of New Mexico ideally. He described the Navajo as great agriculturalists; (no matter that he did not construct churches among the Navajo); Andrés Juárez as the man who had provided for the construction of the Pecos church; and the Pecos Indians who were living with Andres Juárez as models to emulate. During the 1600's, the Spanish Treasury invested 1,340,000 pesos in Spanish religious life across the Spanish Northern Frontier.[18]

The Mexican Inquisition, which had first appeared in New Mexico under the rule of Ysidro Ordóñez, re-appeared in its most benevolent form, with appearance of Custodian or custos, Commissary or comisario and Agent of the Inquisition or agente de la Inquisición Mexicana, Alonso de Benavides in 1626. Due to the amount of work Benavides had to complete in New Mexico, the Inquisition—although there were reasons for it to condemn the governors Juan de Eulate and Felipe Sotelo Osorio in New Mexico and on the future Great Plains—never surfaced, (especially after the fact) during the custos three year term.

---

[18] Weber, David. The Northern Spanish Frontier in North America. Yale University Press. New Haven, Connecct.. 1998} Page 112

The Franciscan Estéban Perea, would be forced in time to defend his bloodlines against the dubious charges of Governor Francisco Mora y Ceballos (1629-32).

Without a doubt, once Estéban Perea had been released from the position of custos of New Mexico, he would be able to accompany, along with the charge of the transportation of Indian slaves (an act which had been banned in New Mexico according to the Recolonization Laws of l573 and would be banned, according to a decree from la Audiencia of Guadaljara in 1660), the departure of Juan de Ulate for Mexico City. Once having survived an appearance in front of el virrey and 2 members of la Audiencia, Ulate was appointed to the governorship of Santa Margarita Island, which to this day we may discover near the coast of Venezuela.

When writing to the Spanish King, Philip IV in 1535, Benavides reconciled, at least from a Franciscan standpoint, the first un-successful tribute collections to have taken from the un-converted pueblos of New Mexico by Juan de Oñate and Pedro de Peralta; to insure the survival of San Gabriel and Santa Fe.

"Through royal decree, it is ordained that no tribute be imposed on the Indians of New Mexico until they have been converted to the Holy Faith. The governor of the province and the custodian must notify el virrey and the Royal Audiencia of Mexico of Mexico, stating the reason they should be imposed; this is to be done by el virrey and the Royal Audiencia and in no other way."[19] Writing with a sense of authority he would not have brought to bear on Governor Felipe Sotelo Osorio (It was not in the character of Benavides to confront secular authority in New Mexico), Benavides suggested to Philip IV; The encomenderos compel the Indians whose house have fallen down or which may have been lost for others reasons to pay tribute even when they live in someone else's house. It is required of your majesty that the Indians of New Mexico do not pay tribute by the person but by the house as has already been done; that as the encomendero is ready to receive tribute added to his pueblos, he should be ready to lose and cease taking tribute from the abandoned houses, even when their owners live in separate houses.'

Having arrived in Santa Fe in January of 1626, Benavides must have had time to observe Governor Eulate's hacienda and the condition of the Pueblo Indians whom had brought it into existence.[20]

Eulate, who was forced to wait until the Fall departure of the New Mexico commissary carts for Mexico City before returning south in 1626, would be brought, under the charges of the Agent of the Inquisition, to trial as a slaver, who had enslaved certain Plains Indians

---

[19]   Kessell, John. Kiva, Cross and Crown. Department of the Interior, Washington D. C. 1979.

[20]   Stanley, Luis. Ciudad Santa Fe. {Denver, Colorado. World Press. 1958.{ Page 66

before appropriating the New Mexico commissary carts for the transport of deer and elk hides, piñón nuts and blankets to the markets of Nueva España and, perhaps, Mexico City.

> It is requested that the governors since your majesty gives them a salary of two thousand ducats a year for their support shall obey la cedula real or Royal Certificate by which they are ordered not to have farms or ranches (Benavides would write to Philip IV in 1631 to laud the Spanish settlement principle in New Mexico) even though They are given a salary for that. This would prevent them from taking the best lands that the Indians have for their fields and depriving the Spaniards of help to develop their lands. And in order to send their cattle to Nueva España to sell they rob the land of cattle which are so desirable for increasing its welfare and permanence. In addition, in order to care for the cattle which then sent to Parral, Nueva Vizcaya, they send along the best Indians who are then left stranded because the distance is so great and they are unable to return home because the distance is so great. It is requested that all caciques, chief-captains, governors on account of the work they perform for the kingdom and your majesty be exempt from tribute and personal service while they maintain these positions. They are so busy in their offices that even their fields are cared for by others. The native lords resent very much that they are compelled to pay tribute. Likewise all Indians who are choir singers and assistants in churches are free from personal service but not from tribute. [21]

The Franciscans, a minor if now hardly a mendicant order in New Mexico (Philip III having taken over the funding of the Franciscans in 1608) had become over and apart from the governor of New Mexico, a series of ecclesiastical laws unto themselves. The institution of tribute would disappear in New Mexico with the foundation of permanent military garrison during the early 1700's.[22]

Although Alonso de Benavides desired to become the first Bishop of New Mexico, he suggested the names of other Franciscans for the position.[23]

---

[21] Kessell, John. Kiva, Cross and Crown. {Washington D. C. Department of the Interior. 1979.} Page 193

[22] Espinosa, J. Crusaders of the Rio Grande.{Chicago, Illinois. Institute of Jesuit History. 1942. P. 345.

[23] Stanley, Francis. {Luís}. Ciudad Santa Fe. The World Press. Denver, Colorado. 1958.

Spanish mysticism whose most remarkable figures—Fray Luís de Leon, Saint John of the Cross and Santa Teresa—contributed to the creation of Spanish letters during the 1500's and beyond—appeared in New Mexico in the form of the Spanish Nun, María Jesús de Ágreda, before the arrival in and after the departure of Alonso de Benavides from New Mexico. According to the Jicarilla Apache and Jumana Indians of New Mexico, a women dressed in the blue clothing of nun had appeared in their camps in order to preach in their languages. The Franciscans of New Mexico did not know for a time what to make of María Jesús de Ágreda.[24]

During the Spring of 1631, the treasury of Nueva España drew up a contract for the provisioning of New Mexico with Fray Tómas Manso, a man of impeccable integrity.[25] Manso was to assure until March 12, 1656, (at which time Fray Juan Ramirez was appointed procurator general of the New Mexico commissary carts) that sixteen, triennial carts (capable of carrying 2 tons of material) left Mexico City for Santa Fe and returned, after a six month lay-over in Santa Fe to Mexico City. If the departure (after 1624) of the commissary carts proved to be advantageous to the Franciscans of New Mexico (Franciscan priests bound for New Mexico received three hundred and twenty-five pesos for expenses and four hundred and twenty-five pesos for three years of service in the field, whereas Franciscan lay-brothers received three hundred and twenty-five pesos for expenses and three hundred pesos for three years of service in the field), the return of the commissary carts proved advantageous to the ex-governors of New Mexico (Juan de Eulate paid his fine and went his way, whereas Diego de Peñalosa fled with information on the Spanish frontier to England and, then, to France) and certain Franciscans numerous of whom replenished their religious and horticultural stock from Nueva Vizcaya. The contents of the New Mexico commissary carts, which left Mexico City for the living sites of Zacatecas, Socorro, Santo Domingo, and, consequently, Santa Fe, served to mirror one of the ecclesiastical motives for the foundation of New Mexico on September 21, 1595. The Pueblo of Santo Domingo {Kewa}was, with the arrival of Alonso Benavides, to become the principal departure point for the Franciscan missionary program across New Mexico. For the provisioning out of and outfitting in of the commissary carts of 1624, on which rode the new governor New Mexico, Felipe Sotelo-Osorio and Custodian, Commissary and Agent of Mexican Inquisition, Alonso de Benavides, we discover:

---

[24] Weber, David,. The Spanish Northern Frontier. Yale University. New Haven, Connect. 1998.

[25] Kessell, John. Kiva, Cross and Crown. (Chicago, Illinois. {Wash. D. C. Department of the Interior. UNM Press. Albuquerque, New Mexico.) Page 222.

107 Mexican blankets

4 fanegas of salt

½ arroba of incense (12 ½ lbs.)

11 henequen socks

26 reams Genoa paper ½ arroba of copal

11 lbs fine linen

26 lbs thread

11 Turkish rugs

10 hats for friars

52 pairs scissors

1 lb. Mixtecan silk

12 traveling bags for bedding

52 pairs Mexican sandals

1 large box wherein which the blessed virgin was housed

11 brevaries

26 hampers in were shipped oil, cheese and ham

11 chausbles[26]

---

[26]   Stanley, Francis. Ciudad Santa Fe. {Denver, Col. World Press. 1958.} Pages 126-27

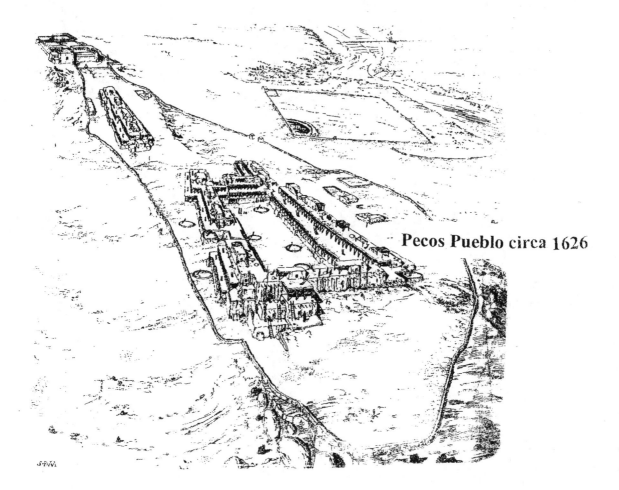

Pecos Pueblo circa 1626

In his revised Memorial of 1634, Benavides wrote:

Al mismo Norte cuatro leguas, se topa con el pueblo de los Pecos, que tiene más de dos mil almas, donde hay un Convento y templo muy lucido, de particular hechura y curiosidad, en que un relgioso puso muy grande trabajo y cuidado y aunque estos indios son de la nación Hémes, por estar aquí solos y desviado de su territorio se tiene por nación aparte, aunque es una misma lengua. Es tierra frigdisima y poco fertile; aunque da el maize suficiente para sus habitadores, porque sembran mucho.

Están estos indios muy bien documentados de todas artes y sus escuelas de leer, escribir, y tañer como los demás.[27]

(Four leagues to the north, one comes in contact with the Pueblo of Pecos, which has approximately two thousand souls and where there is a lucid temple in which a religious one has dedicated a great deal of work. These Indians belong to the Hémez Nation and deflected from the former's territory, remain a nation apart; although the Indians of Pecos and the Indians of Hémez speak the same language. The land is cold and not very fertile; although the Towa of Pecos produce much corn because they sow a great deal. These Indians are very industrialized in all the arts and within their schools of writing, reading, singing and tanning.)

Volviendo del pueblo antecedente hacia el Occidente siete leguas esta la Villa de Santa Fe, cabeza de este reino, donde residen los gobernadores y españoles que serán hasta docientos y cincuenta; aunque solo los cincuenta podran armar por falta de armas y aunque poco y mal aviado, ha permitido Dios que salgan siempre con victoria. Son todos soldados bien documentados y humildes y de Buena ejemplo, por la mayor parte a los indios. A este presidio susetan V. M. no con paga de su caxa real sino, sino haciendolos encomenderos de aquellos por mano del gobernador; el tributo que les dan los indios es cada casa una manta, que es una vara de lienzo de algodón y una fanega de maize cada año, con que se susetan los pobre españoles. Tendrían de servico setecientos almas, de suerte que entre españoles, mestizos e indios habrá mil almas, y gente tan punctual en la obedencia a su gobernador, que a cualquier facción que se ofrezca salen con armas y caballos y su costa y hacen valeroso hechos. Sólo les faltan lo principal que era la iglesia. La que tenían era un jacal malo, porque los religiosos acudían primero a fabricar las iglesias de los indios que convertían y con quienes asistían y vivían asi luego que entre por Custodio commence a fabricar la iglesia y Convento a honra y Gloria de Dios nuestra Señor puede en cualquier parte, a donde los religiosos enseñan los indios a leer, escribir, tañer, todas arte de pulicia. Es puesto aunque frio el más fertile en el Nuevo Mexico.

(Returning from the antecedent pueblo in the direction of west seven leagues is the Villa of Santa Fe; seat of the reign, where live the governors and the Spaniards all of whom reach

---

[27] Ibid

two hundred and fifty although only fifty will be able to arm due to an absence of arms. And although few and poorly supplied, the good fortune of God has always permitted to triumph. They are all good and humble soldiers and serve as examples to the Pueblos. To this pueblo his majesty sustains not with pay from the royal treasury but with tribute, as encomenderos, under the governors from the Pueblos and Hopi Indians. The tribute that the Pueblos give is one cotton blanket, a yard wide and one and one half bushels of corn (twice) a year, in order to support the humble Spaniards. The Villa of Santa Fe contains, among Spaniards, Mestizos and Pueblos nearly thousand persons. The Pueblos are punctual in bravely serving the governor with their presence, arms and horses. All they do not have is the principal which is the church; due largely to the fact that the Franciscans have dedicated themselves to constructing churches in the pueblos; where they teach the Indians to read, write, sing and tan, first before turning to the construction of the church in Santa Fe.)

CHAPTER **VI**

THE NEW MEXICO GOVERNORS DISCOVER THE PROFIT PRINCIPLE

Between 1629 and 1632, the Franciscans suffered human losses in New Mexico due largely to the decision of custos Estéban Perea to assign, with the compliance of Governor Francisco Silva Nieto, Franciscans to the pueblos of the Zuni, the Hopi Pueblo of Awatobi and Keresan Pueblo of Acoma. Between 1629 and 1632, neither the governor nor the Franciscan considered the possible consequences of the expansion of the Franciscan missionary program to the west.

In contrast, the succession of Francisco Mora Ceballos (1632-35) and Francisco Martínez de Baeza (1635-37) to the governorship of New Mexico marked a subtle change (apparent since the reign of Juan de Elate) from the exercise of power over to the acquisition of riches from New Mexico.

Prefiguring the foundation of the Taos trading fairs of the 1720's, (an innovation of Governor Juan Domingo Bustamante (1722-31), the wintering of the Apache in front of Pecos Pueblo had a positive effect on the Spaniards of Santa Fe. During the months of September and October, the Apaches—eco-facts of bone were among the first eco-facts traded into Pecos Pueblo, according to the American archeologist, Alfred Kidder—the Indians of Pecos and the Spaniards of Santa Fe inter-changed trade items, buffalo and deer meat and skins moving from the Apache of the Great Plains to the Towa of Pecos and the Spaniards of Santa Fe and horses and rifles moving from the Spaniards (not without question from the Spaniards) to the Towa of Pecos and the Apache of the Great Plains.[28]

---

[28]   Kessell, John. Kiva, Cross and Crown. Department of the Interior, Washington D. C. 1979.

The Spanish soldier, Luís Rosas, who had distinguished on the fields of Flanders, under the command of el marqués de Caderyeta, became the ninth governor of New Mexico, with ascension of el marqués in question to the Viceroyship of Nueva España or Mexico. Having arrived in Santa Fe within a royal carriage and amidst flageolet or flute, violin and trumpet playing Santa Feans in the Spring of 1637, Rosas was immediately required to conduct a residencia of Governor Francisco Martínez y Baeza. Given in order to determine how responsible the reign of the governors of New Mexico governors had been, la residencia was to take place within the time of one month. In the fall of 1697, former Governor Diego de Vargas remained a free man only during the first thirty days of la residencia he was forced to undergo at the hands of Governor Pedro Rodriquez y Cubero. and the citizens of Santa Fe. Whether Martínez bribed Rosas in order to receive a favorable residencia may be left to conjecture. "Luís Rosas recibió un gran cohecho de su antecessor, Francisco Martínez y Baeza," according to the Franciscans and various settlers of Santa Fe."[29]

As a classic disgusted person (un clásico disgustado), Luís Rosas qualifies as the first would-be reform governor of New Mexico. One day, Rosas simply suggested that the Franciscans give their sheep to the citizens of Santa Fe; the majority of whom had neither weapons sufficient to protect themselves nor material sufficient to clothe themselves.

If Pedro de Peralta had been the first governor to turn the Palace of the Governors into a company store, Luís Rosas was first governor to turn the Palace of the Governors into a factory or fabrica for the production of tapestries, curtains, blankets and candles. As intensely interested in the production of tapestries, curtains, blankets and candles, as he thought his Ute, Apache, and Pueblo Indian workers, ought to be, Rosas worked (although not under the whip) right along side of members of his personal work force.

Luís Rosas was one of the first governors of New Mexico to inaugurate, in his own caravan, two-trade between Mexico City and Santa Fe, arranging for knives, beads, and mirrors worth ten thousand pesos to travel from Mexico City to Santa Fe and tapestries, mantas or blankets, doublets, hose, jackets, deer, beaver and chamois skins to move from Santa Fe to the markets of Nueva Vizcaya.

Early on in his governorship, 'Rosas made an effort to impress the barely impressed Pecos captains not only to deliver their tribute through the window of his Santa Fe abode under

[29]   Stanley, Luis. Ciudad Santa Fe. {Denver, Col. World Press. 1958{ Pages 143, 144, 145.

the cover of night, but to double their tribute in blankets, hides and skins in order that they carry out idolatry in their sect and religion.'[30]

On the other hand, Rosas and his members of the Santa Fe cabildo continued to make impassioned pleas for succor to el virrey. According to the hand-picked members of the Santa Fe cabildo, the Franciscans lorded it over the citizens of Santa Fe, reserving the right to exercise their quasi-episcopal powers, to ex-communicate at will and to extract papal indulgences.[31]

Although Rosas and certain members of the cabildo of Santa Fe continued to make impassioned pleas for succor to the Viceroy in Mexico City, the former's group of followers, which was made up of Friar Vidania and el encomendero and Sergeant-major of Santa Fe, Francsico Goméz y Robledo, who had his house on the plaza, commenced to decrease due to the increase in Rosas's possessions down to fewer and fewer personages of Santa Fe. Goméz y Robledo whose father had been a defender of Governor Juan de Oñate, wrote to el virrey in Mexico City:

> As a result they have this land so afflicted and exhausted that the soldiers despair. This state is easily understood since the religious ones are the masters of the resources and they proceed without a civil judge. The ecclesiastical one they have here is for throwing a cloak over their faults. The faults they possess in this land are not heard beyond this land. And they are not punished with more than a reprimand if one is handed down.[32]

Well after Rosas banished custos Juan Salas from Santa Fe over the questionable death of one of the governor's men who had slandered a friar and almost everyone else who was living in Santa Fe at the time, the Franciscans met at Santo Domingo Pueblo during the Spring of 1641 in order to draw up a manifesto. Having drawn up a manifesto for the approval of the governor, the assembled Franciscans chose 2 unknown Franciscans to walk to Santa Fe in order to present the governor with their perspective of the Franciscans' place in New Mexico. Upon encountering the "messenger friars" awaiting him in front of San Miguel Church,

---

[30]   Kessell, John. Kiva, Cross, and Crown. {Albuquerque, New Mexico, Washington D.. C. Department of the Interior. 1979} page 157

[31]   Ibid.

[32]   Kessell, John. Kiva, Cross and Crown. Department of the Interior, Washington D. C. 1979.

Rosas commenced to berate and to beat either with his cane, or tree branches, the messenger friars from Santo Domingo.[33]

To the degree Rosas contributed to the Taos Rebellion of 1639 and Pueblo Revolt of 1680, is open to conjecture. According to the Franciscans, Rosas encouraged the Tiwa of Taos to deny their "immoral missionary" if not to burn the church of Taos to cinders. Between 1637 and 1641, the correspondence that passed from the governor and his men and el virrey in Mexico City and the correspondence that passed between the Franciscans and el virrey, offers us two diametrically opposed versions of the "events" which took place under the reign of Luís Rosas and the reign of the Franciscans.

In the Spring of 1641, el virrey de Nueva España assigned Juan Flores Sierra y Valdéz to the governorship of New Mexico.[34] Sierra y Valdéz may have arrived in Santa Fe with nothing more than una residencia in his hand. Before the passing away of the governor in question, the citizens of Santa Fe came, with the aid of the governor, into their own, electing the first Democratic representatives or regidores—Francisco Salazar (who would not survive the show trial over the death of Luís Rosas); Juan de Herrera (who would survive the show trail over the death of Luís Rosas); Juan de Archuleta (who would not survive the show trail over the death of Luís Rosas) and Sebastían Gonzalez (who would survive the show trail over the death of Luís Rosas) to the Santa Fe cabildo and subsequently arresting Luís Rosas.[35]

Under orders from Bishop and virrey, Juan Palafox, Juan Pacheco Heredía, the new governor, had 2 tasks to perform. He had to declare, after the taking of the life of Luís Rosas, an amnesty in Santa Fe. Pacheco-Heredía had, as well, to discover the names of the persons who had played a part in the taking of the life of Luís Rosas. Once having discovered (through processes of self-incrimination), the names of the persons who had played a part in the Rosas' drama in Santa Fe, Pacheco-Heredía had the head of the mayor, Antonio Baca, one ring leader of the plan to overthrow Luís Rosas, and the heads of seven soldiers removed over the Santa Fe Plaza.

The Spanish soldier, Nicólas Ortíz, who after having taken, on a pretext, the life of Luís Rosas, had fled earlier to Parral, Chihuahua. From Chihuahua, he was able, after having been arrested for the crime in question, to immigrate safely to Peru in order to live out his life as a vaquero.

---

[33]   Ibid.

[34]   Stanley, Francis. Ciudad Santa Fe. {Denver, Colo. World Press. 1958} Pages 160, 161, 162

[35]   Chávez, Fray Angélico. Origins of Spanish Families in New Mexico. {Santa Fe, New Mexico. Museum of New Mexico Press.} pages 101, 6, 45, 40.

The arrival of Bishop and Viceroy Palafox, who represented religious and royal power and authority in Nueva España and New Mexico appeared not to bode well for the independent Franciscans[36]. The Franciscan religious order, which first came into existence-being under the impetus of Francis Bernadone and with the compliance of the great, in a humanistic sense, Pope Innocent III before Pope Honorious within the town of Assisi, Italy in 1209, provided Franciscans for the Hernando Cortez expedition to Mexico City (1519-1521) and twelve Franciscans for the definite settlement of Mexico City in 1524. With the proclamation of La Ordenanza Patronazgo or Patronage Order by Philip II in 1574, the Franciscans of Mexico would be forced to migrate to the near and distant Spanish frontiers in order to continue with their plans to convert the natives of the New World to Catholicism.

With the announcement of the town crier, Jusepe, to the citizens of Santa Fe for the necessity of the citizens of Santa Fe to pledge allegiance to the Royal Standard, over the Santa Fe Plaza, Bishop Palafox and Governor Pacheco-Heredia had been able to defuse, for a time, the running controversy between the governors and Franciscans over the use of the resources and the Pueblo Indians of New Mexico. Pacheco-Heredía would return, however, to the practice of antagonizing the Franciscans, whereas Bishop Palafox would return, without further ado to Mexico City.

During the reign of Fernando de Arguello (1644-1647), the Pueblo Indians commenced to organize not only under the whips of the Franciscans but because of the presence of the Spaniards in New Mexico.[37]

After the first Jémez revolt, Arguello had twenty-nine Jémez Indians hanged as traitors and confederates of the Apache. In 1650, Pueblo Indian informants informed the Spaniards of Santa Fe of the intent of the Pueblos to round up the horses of Santa Fe just before Holy Thursday. Governor Hernando de Ugarte (1649-1653), with prior knowledge of the intent of the Pueblo Indians, reacted in a similar way, hanging nine leaders of the supposed rebellion.

The Spaniards who were living in New Mexico at the time must have felt secure as long as they knew the intentions of the Pueblo Indians. During the 1600's, New Mexico had six

---

[36] Kessell, John. Kiva, Cross, and Crown. {Albuquerque, New Mexico. Washington D. C. Department of the Interior 1979.} Page 163.

[37] Ibid. Page 1688

alcaldias or mayoral districts under the rule of alcaldes, all of whom had appointed by the governors of New Mexico.[38]

If the shadow of the Mexican Inquisition had fallen over New Mexico with the arrival of Alonso Benavides, the full sun of the Mexican Inquisition would arise over the arrival throughout New Mexico of Governor Bernardo López de Mendízabal in 1659.

If Governor Mendízabal did not want to recognize the religious authority of custos Juan Ramirez, the Franciscans of New Mexico did not want to recognize the secular authority of Governor Mendízabal to govern religious affairs. Mendízabal, who had increased the wage rate of the Pueblo Indians workers of Santa Fe from one half real to one real per day with lunch, made a relative successful effort a well to introduce the idea of wage labor (the Franciscans would go as far as to convene a meeting to determine whether or not Mendízabal's plan merited consideration) to the Pueblo Indians whom were working without remuneration, for the Franciscans of New Mexico.

The Franciscans of New Mexico finally responded to Medízabal's proposal by citing the cédula réal or Royal Certificate of 1646. According to the Franciscans, neither they nor the Pueblo Indians of New Mexico had to pay tribute to the secular authority of New Mexico, even though Mendízabal apparently succeeded with his plan to increase the wage labor rate of the Pueblo Indians of New Mexico. The Pueblo Indians, given a choice of laboring for the Franciscans of New Mexico or returning to their pueblos, chose to leave off working for the Franciscans; thus, contributing to the drought of the 1660's and famine of the 1670's in New Mexico.[39]

Unable to direct traffic in the domain of the Franciscans, Mendízabal wrote to el virrey in Mexico City, accusing them of being "immoral and inhuman."

On the other hand, Mendízabal, sent his mayors who received no official salary to arrange for positions among the Spaniards; to settle water rights between the Puebloans and the Spaniards; and to aid the Franciscans in obtaining Pueblo Indian workers for the day to day upkeep of the Spaniards' churches. The mayors of New Mexico, at least under the reign of Mendízabal, lived on all they were able to draw from the Pueblo Indians and the Franciscans of New Mexico.[40]

---

[38] Hallenbeck, Cleve. Land of the Conquistadors. (Caldwell, Idaho. Caxton Press. 1950) Page 272

[39] Kessell, John. Kiva, Cross and Crown. { Albuquerque, New Mexico. Washington D. C. the Department of the Interior. University of New Mexico Press. 1979.} Page 179.

[40] Linder, Peter. Latin American Studies. Highlands University. Las Vegas, New Mexico. 1992.

With the decision of Governor Mendízabal to arrest Governor Juan Manso (1656-1659), at the conclusion of the latter's residencia of the former, and the appointment, under the auspices of the Holy Office, of Fray Alonso de Posada, as custos and agent of the Mexican Inquisition, the governorship of Governor Mendízabal was on its way if not to a moral to a legal conclusion in Mexico City.

With the appointment of custos Posada, who knew the ground of Santa Fe from before, Mendízabal, as former governor of New Mexico would no longer be able to accuse the Franciscans of New Mexico of 'oppressing mission Indians, misusing their quasi-episcopal powers and immorality (although the Franciscans would continue to collect Indians fetishes).

With the arrest of Mendízabal at the request of the Franciscan Garcia de San Francisco and Diego González Bernal and the subsequent arrest of Mendízabal's men in Santa Fe: Nicólas de Aguilar, alcalde mayor of the Salinas district; Sargento mayor, Diego Romero, former alcalde of Santa Fe; Cristóbal de Anaya Almazán and Francisco Goméz y Robledo, sargento mayor of Santa Fe, by alguacil or sheriff of the Inquisition in New Mexico, Juan Manso, the ecclesiastical and secular powers in Santa Fe coalesced, for a time, in order to defy the rule of former Governor Bernardo López de Mendízabal.[41]

That the arrest of former governor Mendízabal's men was a collective ecclesiastical act motivated, in part, by political motives, seems beyond question. The albeit collective arrest of the fore-mentioned men in question, under the auspices of the Holy Office, points to the accumulative history of the correspondance which had taken place between the Franciscans and the Holy Office and governor and el virrey de Nueva España.

Cristóbal Anaya Almazán and Francisco Goméz y Robledo would in time be cleared of all charges and permitted to return to New Mexico. The collection of encomienda tribute would resume in Santa Fe and would remain to open a rift between Alonso de Posada & Governor Diego de Peñalosa, each of whom desired to collect—the one for the church and other for himself—the tribute of the prisoners in question.

If the office of protector of the Indians had weight only when the Spaniards desired to give it weight, the arrival of the nineteenth governor of New Mexico, Diego Peñalosa, in 1660, and his duty to carry out a residencia (he immediately asked thirty Santa Feans to give him their opinions of the reign of Lopez de Mendízabal), gave the Spaniards who were living in New Mexico at the time sufficient reason not only to name Antonio González Bernal as protector of the Indians but to collect a list of claims against Lòpez de Mendízabal.

---

41   Kessell, John. Kiva, Cross and Crown. {Albuquerque, New Mexico. Department of the Interior. University of New Mexico Press. 1979.} page 176.

Bernardo de Lopez Mendízabal was forced to reimburse himself for having had to pay his way into the governorship of New Mexico to become a businessman of the first order. Juan de Oñate, who paid 500,000 ducats in order to outfit out his settlement expedition to New Mexico, was not a businessman. Diego de Vargas, who paid five thousand escudos to the Spanish Treasury to become the twenty-eight governor of New Mexico would in time have to spend between thirty to forty thousand pesos of his own in order to insure the re-settlement of Santa Fe for the Spaniards.

Mendízabal, upon receiving the judgments of the Mexican Inquisition {guilty on sixteen of thirty-three counts which had been brought against him by González—Bernal and, apart from two hundred and forty counts the Franciscans of New Mexico would have like to have brought against the governor}, was transferred to a Spanish prison in Mexico City. The Mexican Inquisition, having reached New Mexico for the third time, had become transferred into the due process of law common to New Mexico.

With the impounding of the goods of former governor Mendízabal in Parral, Nueva Vizcaya, by custos Posada (the arrival in New Mexico on May 9, 1661, had preceded the arrival of Governor Peñalosa in New Mexico by three months) and the former's collection of the tribute of Francisco Goméz y Robledo in the Spring of 1662, the stage was set for a series of confrontations between custos Posada and Governor Peñalosa.

Diego Penalosa was, as the first Portuguese to come to the governorship of New Mexico (1661-1664), in a position to take over the material inheritance of López de Mendízabal. Having acquired through a series of go-between debt collectors the material inheritance of López de Mendízabal, Peñalosa set out to intimidate custos Alonso Posada. Having ordered the arrest of a local rancher over his questionable acquisition of livestock, Peñalosa refused the former asylum in the church of Santo Domingo.[42]

Upon hearing of incident in question, custos Posada wrote a letter to Governor Peñalosa, demanding asylum for the rancher in question. Peñalosa, reacting to an affront to his authority, rode out to Pecos Pueblo in order to place under arrest, custos Posada.

Having returned to Santa Fe to the closure of the convent of Santa Fe, Governor Peñaslosa and custos Posada entered the Casa Real (with a cannon trained on its doorway and a gibbet erected in the plaza) in order to commence a series of discussions over the respective jurisdictions of the state and church in New Mexico

---

42   Scholes France. The New Mexico Historical Review. 1932.

General Don Diego, continuing with his replies and propositions, said to me, "Why is your reference trying ex-communicate me for having ordered Don Pedro de Chávez taken from the church at Santo Domingo and held prisoner.

I replied, "Sir, as an ecclesiastical judge I am obliged to defend the immunity of the Church, and because terms had not been reached for proceeding in the matter judicially, I wrote 2 letters of supplication to your Excellency, who up to now, is not ex-communicate or declared as such. And with regard to the case concerning immunity, you may state through your attorney, proceeding in legal form the reasons you had for removing him. And if the reasons of your Lordship were sufficient for doing so, there is no controversy because the case is one of those contained in the law, as will be seen in the second part of the Decretls, in quest. Cap. 8, 9, 10. If the case is carried to the use of force, it is really not necessary, even symbolically, to hang the pontiff of the Catholic Church.[43]

One reason why custos Posada was successful in defending himself during his discussions with Governor Peñalosa may have been due to the fact that Posada never crossed beyond the line of truth set, according to his character, for the encounter in question. Peñalosa belied his judicial impotence more than once in his encounter with Posada, brandishing his pistols in the face of the custos at Pecos Pueblo.

After seven days of discussions, Governor Peñalosa opened the front door of la Casa Réal to the safe departure of custos Posada.

Once having ordered the opening of the convento de Santa Fe, essentially to allow Governor Peñalosa to receive the sacraments, custos Posada brought, against the former and for the Mexican Inquisition, charges of the appropriation of the material goods of Nuevo Mexicanos, the opening of Inquisición mail and the arrest of the custos New Mexico.

Given it would take 2 days to present to el virrey and 2 members of la Audiencia, the charges which had been brought by custos Posada and the Franciscans against former governor Peñalosa. Peñalosa was subsequently banned from New Mexico and Nueva España for life. The Spanish and Portuguese governors of New Mexico had been for time dependent on knowledge that they had acquired largely from Pueblo informants of the organizational tendencies of the Pueblo Indians. Without a doubt, the governors of New Mexico,

---

43   Kessell, John. Kiva, Cross, and Crown. {Albuquerque, New Mexico. Washington D. C. Department of the Interior. 1979.} Page 205

Franciscans, soldier-settlers and settler soldiers had taken advantage of and provided for the Pueblo Indians of New Mexico during the middle and late 1600's. The Pueblo Indians of New Mexico would be for time wholly dependent on the Spanish community; the cause and, to various degrees, solution to the question of drought across New Mexico during the 1660's. {See statement of Governor Bernardo López de Mendízabal, to the effect}.

During the drought of the 1660's and the subsequent famine of the 1670's across New Mexico, the Pueblo Indians would suffer hunger, disease and loss at the hands of the Apache raiders far out of proportion to the losses of life and property the Spaniards would suffer at the hands of the Apache and natural effects of drought and famine over the landscape of New Mexico during the same time period.

Even though governors such as Francisco Villanueva (1665-1668) and Juan de Medrano (1668-1671) would appear to be on good terms with the Franciscans of New Mexico, the material wealth of the Franciscans would prevent them from outfitting out either New Mexico governor's men or his Indian auxiliaries.

If Governor Villanueva had made requisitionary demands on custos Talában, custos Talában agreed, in spirit, with the necessity to protect New Mexico but not without a guarantee for the replacement of the horses and mules that could be lost in campaigns against the Apache.[44]

---

[44]   Hallenbeck Cleve. Land of the Conquistadores. Caxton Press. Caldwell, Idaho. 1950.

CHAPTER VII

THE PUEBLO REVOLT OF 1680

Governor Antonio Otermín (1677-1683), who came to New Mexico on the commissary caravan of 1677, inherited not only a drought ridden royal colony, but the tendency, (Spanish since the onset of drought in during the 1660's) of the governors and the Franciscans to agree on certain unifying principles for the preservation of Spanish and Indian life in New Mexico. According to the Franciscan, Francisco de Ayeta, Otermín had set out, almost on arrival in New Mexico, to stock with provisions the southern New Mexico pueblo of Senecú.

Fray Ayeta, who had been selected by el virrey to take over, inside and outside of the time set aside for the New Mexico commissary carts, the provisioning of New Mexico in 1674, was for a time the only Nuevo Mexicano to look south in order to make an effort to ease the drought of the 1660's and subsequent famine of the 1670' across New Mexico;.

If Otermín had set out to re-stock certain pueblos of the Rio Grande from the outset of his entry into New Mexico, he would soon distance himself from having to rule the Pueblos of New Mexico, leaving the question of "enforcing discipline" to his maeses del campo or master of the camp, Francisco Javier. The Spaniard's efforts to discipline the Pueblo Indians of the eras in question would succeed only with the entry of Diego de Vargas into Santa Fe.

Francisco Javier, who had been the secretary of Governor Francisco Treviño, inherited the Spanish legacy of the suppression of witchcraft and certain Pueblo Indians who had been convicted of practicing witchcraft among the Tewa Pueblos. As the inheritor of the Spanish custom of hanging Indian conspirators, Governor Trevino (1675-77) had, in the first year of his reign, three Pueblo Indians hanged (another hanged himself) for supposedly contributing to the passing of the Franciscan Andrés Duran at San Ildefonso Pueblo. One of the forty-three Indians who had been arrested, whipped and, then, released, was Popé, a shamán or religious leader from San Juan Pueblo.

Prior to the outbreak of the Pueblo Revolt of 1680, Francisco Javier had, as master of the camp or maeses del campo and second in command to Governor Treviño, spent his time, apart from collecting Pueblo fetishes, rhapsodizing over the state of the military across the Spanish Empire. Neither Treviño nor Javier would be prepared for the arrival in Santa Fe, shortly after the arrest of the shaman in question, of a delegation of seventy Pueblo Indians. To the Pueblo demand for the release of the Pueblo shaman and at the reception of a gift of eggs, Trevino reportedly said: "Wait a while children and I will given them to you on condition that you forsake idolatry and iniquity."[45]

The Franciscan, Fernando de Velasco, guardian and friar of Pecos Pueblo, had received notification {as he had without result numerous times before} from Governor Juan Yi of Pecos, of an impending revolt of the Pueblo Indians on August 8, 1680; 2 days before the day which had been set aside for the uprising of the Pueblo Revolt, by either Popé or el Naranjo, a huge black mulatto with yellow eyes whose antecedents had accompanied the Governor Juan de Oñate expedition to New Mexico in 1589 before settling, as wrangler of horses and cattle, in Santa Clara Pueblo.

"Padrecito la gente se va sublevar y matar todos los españoles y missioneros." Little father the people are going to rise up and kill all the Spaniards and missionaries. "Decidid ahora si queries alejar. Os daré guerreros para su protección." Decide now if you want to distance yourself. I shall give you warriors for you protection.[46]

Although Governor Otermín had received knowledge of the 2 young Tesuque runners, Catua y Omtua, each of whom had been chosen by Popé to notify the Pueblos of an impending revolt, the governor, remaining in the steps of Fernando de Velasco, refused to believe in the potential for a pueblo revolt.

When news of the imminence of the Pueblo Revolt of 1680 began to seep into Santa Fe on August 10, 1680, Otermín ordered the fortification of Las Casas Réales or Royal Houses and La Casa Réal or Governors Palace.

The Pueblo Revolt of August 9-21, 1680, in which up to 3,000 Pueblo and Apache Indians took the lives of approximately three hundred and eighty Spaniards and twenty-one

[45] Kessell, John. Kiva, Cross and Crown. {Albuquerque, New Mexico. Department of the Interior. University of New Mexico Press 1979.} Pages 226-27

[46] Chávez, Fray Angélico. The Origins of Spanish Families in New Mexico. Museum of New Mexico Press.

Franciscans, clarified as never before the relations which were to develop between the Pueblo Indians and the Spaniards who would come to live in New Mexico during the 1700's. The effects of the Pueblo Revolt—the final disappearance of la encomienda and, eventually, el repartimiento and the decision of the Pueblo Indians to create, along with the Spaniards, common cause against certain Apache, Navajo and Comanche and the assimilation of the members of the Pueblos and Genizaros (captured Plains Indians); into the communities of New Mexico, would be far greater than the causes of the Pueblo Revolt of 1680.

During the winter of 1681, Governor Otermín made an effort, with his retinue of soldiers, servants and Indian auxiliaries, to return and re-conquer New Mexico for the Spaniards. Upon returning to New Mexico on a "search and inquiry mission," Otermín interviewed various Pueblo Indians, burned several abandoned pueblos; and sent a reconnaissance expedition, under Juan Dominguez de Mendoza, north from Ysleta Pueblo with hope of making contact with the Pueblo Indians; numerous of whom may have set out under Alonso Catatí to act in bad faith. Having been unable to make contact with the Pueblo Indians beyond Ysleta (the majority of the Northern Tiwa of Alameda, Sandia, and Puarai, had taken questionable, due to the weather and hunger, refuge in the future Sandia mountains), Otermin's reconnaissance expedition, the majority of whose leaders had met, to discuss strategy, at the hacienda of Luis Mejia, decided (after and apart from Dominguez de Mendoza's suggestion to advance to Santo Domingo Pueblo) to return to Ysleta Pueblo and, consequently, through snow storms to Paso del Norte on February 7, 1682.[47]

With the succession of Domingo de Cruzate to the governorship of New Mexico in 1683, the phenomenal luck of the Spaniards held, due largely to the Apache dominance if not take over of Santa Fe and the uprising of the Manso, Julimes and Janos tribes to the south, southwest and west of Paso del Norte.[48]

The Pueblo Indians of New Mexico who had moved into Santa Fe after the successful Pueblo Revolt of 1680 had soon discovered themselves to be subjects of the Apaches use of force, demand for tribute labor, and acquisition of Tlaxcalan Indians from Barrio of Analco. Rather than see Pueblo farmers shot down on their way to the Pueblo corn fields of Santa Fe, the Pueblo Indians of Santa Fe adapted to the demands of the Apache. Unable to rule Santa Fe in accord with one another, the Pueblo Indians of Santa Fe adopted the outer living

[47]   Hackett, Charles Wilson (editor) and Charmion Clair Shelby (translator). Revolt of the Pueblo Indians of New Mexico and Otermín's Attempted Reconquest, 1680-1682. (Albuquerque: The University of New Mexico Press, 1942). Volume 9, pages 232-253.

[48]   Stanley, Francis. {Luís}. Ciudad Santa Fe. The World Press. Denver, Colorado. 1958.

quarters of the Spaniards that had been constructed around the Santa Fe Plaza before taking up Pueblo inner roles as settled farmers of Santa Fe.[49]

Having been encouraged to rebel by the triumph of the Pueblo Indians over the Spaniards of New Mexico, the Julimes, Manso and Janos Indians of northern Nueva Vizcaya, set out (without realizing that they would be) like the Pueblo Indians of New Mexico had been, subjects of Pueblo Indian informants, to annihilate the Spaniards who were living at the time within Paso del Norte. Reacting in a foreseeable way to information provided by Pueblo Indian informants, Cruzate had eight leaders of the proposed revolt hanged, thus setting the stage for uprisings in the Casas Grandes and Janos districts and their subsequent de-ignition by Spanish forces from Paso del Norte.

While the Pueblo historian, Joe Sando, thinks it incomprehensible that Governor Cruzate should have conceded Pueblo Indian lands, in the form of land grants, to the Pueblo Indians, had he not done so, the American legal system may not have recognized the Pueblo Indians' rights to Pueblo Indian land. [50]

With on-set of drought in Paso del Norte district, Cruzate ordered the reduction of the distance between the Paso del Norte Presidio and the local communities of Ysleta, Soccoro and San Lorenzo.

Bartolomé de Ojeda of Zia and Santa Ana Pueblos had been among the first Pueblo Indians to have successfully fought against the Spaniards who had raided his pueblo. Accompanying the force (the Vargas expedition of 1692) was a very important Pueblo Indian, Bartolomé de Ojeda. Fray Silvestere Escalante later noted that his Sia warrior had fought very well against the Spanish soldiers who had attacked Zia. Ojeda was muy Ladino or fluent in the Spanish tongue and knew how to read and write). Not only was he valuable as an interpreter for the Spaniards but he was at all times reliable as an informant concerning the state of affairs among the Indians.[51]

Ojeda had been wounded in the fire-fight under Govenor Cruzate, at Sia in 1689, and consequently, transferred to Paso del Norte.[52]

Governors Domingo Petríz de Cruzate and Pedro Reneros de Posada each epitomized, perhaps, the Spanish conquest principle (without reconciliation) of the era in question.

---

[49] Ibid.

[50] Sando, Joe. The Pueblo Nation. {Santa Fe, New Mexico. Clear Light Publishing. 1992.} page 67.

[51] Espinosa, J. Crusaders of the Rio Grande. Institute of Jesuit Studies. Chicago, Illinois. 1942.

[52] Fray Silvestre Velez de Escalante. Extracto de Notaciones. Archivos de Santa Fe. 1788. Espinosa, J. Pueblo Indian Revolt of 1696. Chicago, Illinois. 1942} Page 36

CHAPTER VIII

THE ENTRY OF GOVERNOR DIEGO DE VARGAS INTO SANTA FE

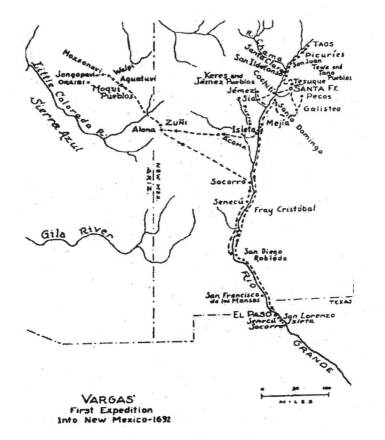

VARGAS'
First Expedition
Into New Mexico-1692

The idea of re-conquest, the essential motive for the re-entry of the Spaniards into New Mexico, at least within the minds of the Spanish King Carlos II (1665-1700), Governor Antonio Otermín (1677-1683), Governor Domingo de Cruzate (1683-86) (1689-91), and Governor Pedro de Posada,(1686-89) would evolve into being one of re-conquest and reconciliation, to a series of points, with entry of Diego de Vargas' reconnaissance expedition which numbered forty Spaniards, ten militia men and fifty Indians from Paso del Norte district into the environs of Santa Fe on 13 September, 1692.

The entry of Governor Vargas into the environs of Santa Fe on September 13, 1692, provides us with not only the constants, such as Spanish law, but certain rational, logical and reasonable variables, such as forgiveness, safe conduct, and sense of community with which he would make an effort to reconcile the immediate and eventual acceptance of the Pueblo Indians to the return of the Spaniards to New Mexico. Vargas' Journal entry of 13 September states:

> I then resumed the march as far as the foot of meadow and open country; where I discovered that I was but a quarter of a league from the villa. At this point, I again stopped to assemble the soldiers. Gathered there I told them that my order to them was to enter the square and while there, in view, of and near the apostates, treacherous rebels have in their pueblo, the whole camp was to shout out three times: 'Glory be to the Blessed Sacrament of he Altar.' No one was to give battle. That the friendly Indians allies with me might understand this I had an interpreter tell them of my wishes.[53]

Vargas' Journal entry of September 13, 1692, shows him to have been a man of faith who had entered into a state of siege in order to besiege with men, cannon and mortar if necessary, the fortress of Santa Fe. With the break of dawn and the chanting of prayers, Vargas alone with 2 other men (Vargas alone would rule Santa Fe with aid of this "servants" and future governors, Juan Páez Hurtado and Antonio Valverde) approached the entrance to the fortress of Santa Fe, giving voice to his desire to re-acquire Santa Fe for the Spaniards.

Once having been asked to play the "Clarion," a trumpet call, by one of the chief spokespersons for the Pueblo Indians of Santa Fe, Vargas responded with 'not only will I play the clarion but I will beat a war drum.'

---

[53]   Kessell, J. By Force of Arms: The Journals of Don Diego de Vargas, 1691-1693. University of New Mexico Press; 1st edition (July 1, 1992).

At this point in the negotiations, the Tano and Tewa defenders of Santa Fe began to shout the Spaniards down and deploy in defense of Santa Fe. Briefly undone by his temerity, Vargas developed a more conciliatory tone. "Listen to me, I have come in the name of our king and master. He bids me pardon you in his name. become Christians as you formerly were. Do not remain under the power of the devil. Do you not recognize the queen of queens, our lady, the blessed virgin?"

A Pueblo chief made, from within the walls of Santa Fe, a largely unsuccessful effort to remind Vargas of the accord making tendencies, under Alonso Benavides and the according breaking tendencies, under Felipe Sotelo-Osorio, of the Spaniards whom had lived in Santa Fe. Vargas countered the charge, which was true, with tact and reassurance, (he knew the history of the New Mexico governors) assuring the Pueblos that the Spaniards who had killed Apache on the Great Plains were not with him.

Having removed a rosary from his coat with one hand and raised on his stirrup a banner of the virgin on one side and the king on the other, Vargas implored the Pueblos to accept the rule of the Spaniards over Santa Fe. With the arrival and positioning of the Spaniards' artillery pieces, over the Santa Fe Plaza, Vargas came away from the walls of Santa Fe in order to have an early lunch with the Franciscans of Santa Fe.

With the return of Vargas to the Plaza de las Armas or the Santa Fe Plaza, the chief spokesperson for the Pueblos demanded that the Spaniards remove their artillery pieces from the Santa Fe Plaza. Vargas responded to this demand by diverting the water-way which had up to the led to the fortress of Santa Fe. Neither the Spaniards of 1680 nor the Pueblos of 1692 had made provision for the storage of water.

Before departing from the Santa Fe Plaza, Vargas left the Pueblo Indians with a final order; 'I am going to supper, by the time I return I expect you all to be wearing little crosses of peace. I also wish to see a large cross in the center of the plaza. Here, it is imperative to understand the symbolic import of Vargas' request.

As Vargas was eating supper, he ordered the Spanish artillery to be removed from the Santa Fe Plaza and the night watch doubled over the Spaniards' horses. The very next morning, Vargas encountered, upon entering the Santa Fe Plaza, a cross approximately 3 meters in elevation, standing along with ten Pueblo Indians in the center of the Plaza. As if by an act of sympathetic magic, the ten pueblo Indians had become hundreds.

A master rhetorician, Vargas never lost control of his rhetorical or his tactical edge over the Pueblo Indians of Santa Fe between September 13 and September 14, 1692. Vargas and his forces accomplished the military conquest of Santa Fe without the loss of a single Pueblo or Spanish life.

Having set out on whirlwind tour of the Pueblos of New Mexico, largely without the presence of Luis Tupatú, who had just come down, at the request of the governor of Pecos, Juan Yi, from Ohkay Owingeh, to confer with the Spaniards, Vargas first tempered (imprisoning and, the, releasing thirty-four Indians of Pecos) the familial presence as well as the warrior absence of the Towa of Pecos on September 19, 1692. Vargas would in time write in his Journal: 'I, the governor was unable to carry out the reduction and bringing together of the Indians of Pecos in their Pueblo.' Having celebrated the Feast of the Archangel Michael on September 20, 1692, Vargas entered the Pueblos of Tesuque, three leagues to the north of Santa Fe on September 30, 1692. In order to meet with his compadre Governor Domingo Uguarte, who had scouted Pecos for the Spaniards. Once having had the members of Tesuque assemble in the plaza of Tesuque, Vargas informed, through the Spanish interpreter, Pedro de Hidalgo, the Tewa of Tesuque of the essential national and religious motives for the Spaniards' re-conquest of New Mexico.

> After short time as I was in the plaza, I called the Indian Domingo and ordered him to assemble all of his people, telling them that I was ordering them to come down. When that was done, I had the alfárez réal go out with a squadron of soldiers and military leaders, ordering them to form a rank with only their swords, facing the Indians. I took the position in the center, ordering the interpreter and my secretary to be present, I told the interpreter that he should state in the language the Indians speak that I had come from far away to see them by order of the king who was theirs and no other. I told them through the interpreter what was referred to, which is of record in the proceedings of 14 September in the Villa of Santa Fe. Revalidating and reclaiming the possession that his majesty, the king, our lord, (may god keep him), has of this Pueblo, land and its inhabitants, who are his vassals. As a sign, I ordered the alfárez réal to raise the royal standard three times, with everyone repeating three times: "Long live the king our lord, Carlos II, king of all the Spains, this new world and the kingdom of New Mexico that has been reduced and conquered for his royal crown and our holy faith whose vassals these are. Everyone answered with much rejoicing and happiness. 'Viva many time and may good fortune of his Monarchy increase.' After that was said, I told them through the interpreter, Pedro Hidalgo, that I was bringing the reverend missionary fathers with me so they might absolve them of the great sin that they had committed during uprising. By virtue of this pardon, I had brought image of the blessed virgin on the royal standard, which I showed them. The Franciscans also baptized all the boys and girls and infants. I, the

governor and captain-general, was god father to a daughter of Captain Domingo, as well as the people who gave their children so that I might take and hold them, so that they might be baptized. The leaders, soldiers and other persons did likewise, Seventy-four boys and girls were baptized.[54]

Upon his entry into the Pueblos of Cuyamungé, Nambé and Pojoaqué on 30 September, Jacona and San Ildefenso on October 1st, and Santa Clara Pueblo on October 2nd respectively, Vargas repeated the successful process of "conquest and conversion" that he had practiced among the Tewa of Tesuque.

In order to honor the arrival of Vargas and his forces into Ohkay Owingeh or San Juan pueblo, Luís Tupatu, one of the leaders of the Pueblo Revolt of 1680 and spokesperson for the Tewa and Tano of northern New Mexico, met Vargas and his forces one league in front of San Juan or Ohkay Owingeh Pueblo on October 2nd, 1692. After having given his re-conquest speech, Vargas requested that the Franciscan Corvera absolve all of those Tewa present who had been living during the Pueblo Revolt of 1680 as well as those Tewa children whom had been born since the Pueblo Revolt of 1680. Vargas discovered as well 2 Spanish women who had been living with the Tewa of Ohkay Owingeh.

Having ordered on October 3, 1692, "his camp and his men" to remain at San Juan, Vargas and 2 squads of ten men each and the Franciscan Francisco Corvera and Cristóbal Barroso, set out (most tentatively) according to his Journal, for San Lázaro and San Cristóbal Pueblos.

Upon reaching the Pueblo of San Cristóbal, Vargas revalidated the possession and reduction of said Pueblo to the rule of the Spaniards, arranging for the re-unification of certain Puebloans who had been separated during the Pueblo Revolt of 1680 and bringing briefly into question the idea of Spanish canón law in as much as it related to married couples in New Mexico.

Having entered the Pueblo of Sán Lázaro during the afternoon of October 3rd, 1692, Vargas and his men met with Tano capitán Cristóbal Yopé. Yopé was to subsequently to ease the "the religious reduction and military re-conquest" of said pueblo before presenting his daughter in the form of a grand-child to Vargas. Without the presence of either cannon or stone mortar (due to the nature of the terrain), Vargas was forced to enter, under the authority of Luis Tupatú, Tewa leader of the Northern Pueblos of New Mexico and Picuran

---

[54]   Kessell, J. By Force of Arms: The Journals of Don Diego de Vargas, 1691-1693. University of New Mexico Press; 1st edition (July 1, 1992).

41

Lorenzo Tupatú. Picuríes. Having successfully entered, under his credo of "convince and convert" in contrast to Antonio Otermín's credo of "search and inquire" and departed from the Pueblo Picuríes on October 6, 1692, Vargas, reached Taos Pueblo the next day if not those pueblo leaders whose forces had been raiding the pueblos of New Mexico.

Once having discovered Taos pueblo, which had been deserted since news of the entry of the Spaniards into Santa Fe had reached the northern pueblos of New Mexico, Vargas sent Luís and Lorenzo Tupatú to look for the Tiwa of Taos at the entrance to their mountain retreat. With subsequent intervention of one Taos brave who had descended from the Taos mountain retreat in order to treat with the Spaniards of Santa Fe, the Tewa of San Juan and the Tiwa of Picuríes, Vargas succeeded in talking the Tiwa of Taos down out of the mountains and into the Tewa and Tiwa ambeance of Taos for the first time. For this act, Vargas would petition for the honorific or honorifico de márques.

Once having "re-validated and re-conquered" the Pueblos of New Mexico—he would eventually receive the accord of twenty-three Pueblos of future New Mexico and Arizona between 13 September and 23 October 1692—Vargas sent complete accounts of his exploits to el virrey, el Conde de Galve, on October 16, 1692.

Upon the reception of a letter dated November 23, 1692, from el Conde de Galve, y la Junta General de la Ciudad de Mexico, Vargas was given full rein (after his original plan) to re-organize his definitive settlement expedition to New Mexico. The very day after his return to Paso del Norte, Vargas made plans to conduct a census count, in order, perhaps, to affirm the knowledge that he had had of the settlers of Paso del Norte.

Although el Conde de Galve had given Vargas permission to recruit, for his settlement expedition, potential as well as former settlers of Santa Fe, from Parral, Durango, Sombrerte, and Zacatecas, the latter, after having discovered the one thousand persons who were living Paso del Norte without the means to support themselves, requested, within his letter to el virrey, of January 12, 1693, five hundred families, one hundred soldiers and additional funds beyond the recent issuance of twelve thousand pesos (he would receive forty thousand from the treasures of Zacatecas, Durango and Sombrerete). The Vargas expedition, which would be composed of eighteen Franciscans, twenty-seven mestizos and mulatto families, sixty-three Spanish families, three Frenchmen and at least one Pueblo Indian, set out for Santa Fe on 4 October 1693.

CHAPTER **IX**

THE SPANIARDS' RE-CONQUEST OF SANTA FE

Having arrived in front of Santa Fe Vargas, along with the members of his expedition, was forced to endure the cold and snows of the Santa Fe Winter as well as reductions in his food supply. Governor Juan Yi of Pecos stocked the Spaniards with 8 fanegas (12 bushels of maize) and four fanegas (6 bushels of flour). Unsuccessful in his effort to have the Tano and Tewa defenders of Santa Fe return to their Pueblos, Vargas and Spanish, Paso del Nortean and Pueblos forces successfully stormed (after protracted negotiations dating from approximately the December 15th) the fortress of Santa Fe on December 29, 1693. With the return of Vargas and his settlement expedition, the tortilla had turned over for the Spaniards of New Mexico; as the idea of one person taking advantage of another will have evolved from being dependent on the person to become to being dependent on the condition to create in New Mexico. Upon securing Santa Fe, Vargas had only to await the arrival of Governor Juan Yi of Pecos. Yi, the second Pueblo governor to have given himself over to the Spaniards (Bartolomé de Ojeda having been the first), desired to assure the place of Pecos Pueblo as the major trading center in New Mexico, whereas the Apache traders desired to renew trade with the Spaniards of Santa Fe. Yi, Vargas and the Apache traders saw Santa Fe at this moment in time for the first time.

With the triumph of the Vargas expedition, approximately one hundred Indians from the Paso del Norte district and the Indians of Pecos over the Tano and Tewa Indian language groups of Santa Fe, Vargas decided to act on his own and seemingly apart from the Council of Indies, distributing temporarily for work and culturalization, over two hundred Puebloans all of who had surrendered to the settlers of Santa Fe and immediately taking (with thoughts, perhaps, of the Spaniards who had lost their lives in the cold in front of Santa Fe the lives of fifty-four Puebloans all of whom had gone into hiding in the fortress of Santa Fe).

The centri-petal or inner psychical and physical direction presence of the members of Pecos, San Felipe, Santa Ana and Sia Pueblos would more than counter-balance, however, the centri-fugal or outer psychical direction presence of most members of the pueblos of Tesuque, Nambé, Pojoaqué, Cuyamungé, Jacona, Santa Clara, San Ildefenso, Santo Domingo, Jémez, Acoma, San Cristóbal, San Lázaro, Picuríes and Taos during the resistance of the Pueblos thorughout 1694 and the Pueblo Revolt of 1696.

Only a few Pueblo Indians defenders of Santa Fe may have escaped the re-entry of the Spaniards into Santa Fe on December 29, 1693 (New Mexico historians differ as to the exact number and Vargas' decision not to follow up the rumor that the Spaniards of Santa Fe were going to take the lives of the male members of the Pueblos.) That Vargas did not immediately set out to re-assure the Pueblos of the Spaniards' intentions remains an open question for New Mexico historians to consider.

Having triumphed over the Tano and Tewa of Santa Fe, Vargas renewed his request to el virrey el Conde de Galve for three hundred and twenty families to be sent immediately to Santa Fe, largely in order to justify the Spaniards' settlement principle in New Mexico. For the consideration of el Conde de Galve, Vargas requested, for immediate departure for Santa Fe, six thousand head of cattle, four thousand mules, five thousand mares, five hundred stallions, five hundred plowshares; five hundred axes five hundred sheep, five hundred hoes and five hundred iron spades.

El virrey Galve, a Vargas man with limited resources, in Mexico City, responded to Vargas' quest by authorizing the departure of sixty-six and on half families from Mexico City, the majority of whom after their arrival in Santa Fe on June 23rd, 1694 would settle in Santa Cruz de la Cañada.

During late January of 1694, Vargas and sixty individuals from Santa Fe set out in the direction of San Ildefenso Pueblo. Traveling north, the Spaniards came to Tesuque Pueblo, which had been abandoned to ample stores of maize or corn. Upon entering Nambé Pueblo, Vargas and his men encountered one half dozen Pueblo Indians who upon "dismounting form their horses had made for the near-by mountains." The Spaniards discovered the houses of Nambé to be full of maize. Upon the arrival of the Spaniards in San Ildefenso Pueblo, Vargas ordered his men to take up positions within the Pueblo in question before bedding down in its environs. Once having released prisoners in the direction of San Ildefenso Mesa or Black Mesa, Vargas had only to await the arrival of a messenger from the assembled Tewa and Tano of Black Mesa. With the arrival of Pueblo informant named Nicólas, the assembled Tano and Tewa defenders of San Ildefenso Mesa renewed their request for Vargas and the Franciscan, Alpuente, to ascend to the top of Black Mesa. Wary of the intentions of the Tewa and Tano defenders of Black Mesa, Vargas planted a cross in the center of San Ildefenso Pueblo before returning to Santa Fe.

Upon his arrival in Santa Fe, Vargas once having been apprised of the desire of the Keresasn of Cochití to intervene in the lives of the independent Keresan of Sia, Santa Ana and San Felipe, made plans to set out to reach the Cochití Mesas of Cieneguilla. In early April, Vargas ordered his second in command, Roque de la Madrid to organize ninety soldiers, twenty militia men and 2 standard bearers and 2 others for immediate departure in the direction of Cochití Mesa.

Having arrived in front of Cochití Mesa on April 17, 1694, Vargas was this time (the Spaniards had been unable to surround the Tano and Tewa of San Ildefenso Mesa due to its immense size) able to deploy in three separate columns from three separate directions, achieving relatively easily under rains of arrows and sling stones, the top of San Ildefenso Mesa.

Having captured, almost intact, the Keresan of Cochití, Vargas ordered the lives of thirteen leaders taken, three hundred and forty-two prisoners placed under guard and seventy horses and mules and nine hundred sheep (at least half of which belonged to the Spaniards) set aside for delivery to Santa Fe. Awaiting for el Río Grande in flood to subside, Vargas sent a squad of soldiers to guard the farmers of San Felipe as they set out to plant their Spring crops for Fall harvest. Upon arrival in Santa Fe, Vargas requested that the Spaniards of Santa Fe plant "three suertes" or gardens for the fall harvest of ten fanegas of maize.

Upon his return to Santa Fe on May 2nd, 1694, Vargas had met with various Apache traders from the future Great Plains, all of whom seemed of late to appear between the Spaniards battle for allegiance of the independent Pueblos of New Mexico In order to appear in good faith within the eyes of Vargas, the Apache traders presented the Spaniards of Santa Fe with "one elk-skin camp tent" and buffalo hides," promising to return in the fall when the maize was ripe. Vargas with one eye on the non-existent blue lake, presented the Apache with a silver plate in order to request information on the nature of silver or "white-iron." The Apache responded to Vargas' request in the affirmative, stating that they had seen it, but had been unable to remove from their native lands due to its extreme weight.

With all due respect for the Rio Grande in flood, Vargas and fifty men from Santa Fe and his Indian auxiliarios, attentive as always to the counsel of Juan Yi of Pecos, set out north along the Santa Fe side of the Río Grande on June 30, 1694, for the grain laden pueblos of northern New Mexico. Having had to fend off an attack near Cuyamungé, the Vargas expedition camped across from Black Mesa before continuing through the deserted for a time sites of San Cristóbal, San Lázaro, the hacienda of Moraga and Picuríes Pueblo.

Directly ahead, beyond a mountain valley, lay Taos Pueblo. Having pulled up near the cultivated fields and in front of the branch of the river that leads near the entrance to Taos Pueblo, Vargas, with complete knowledge of the terrain ordered, Governor Juan Yi and Sergeant Antonio Jorge, to search for the Tiwa of Taos at the entry way to their mountain retreat.

Without either the consideration or caution of Vargas, Yi, upon meeting with the Tiwa of Taos, volunteered to parley overnight with Governor Pacheco of Taos. The next day, Vargas waited in vain for ether Juan Yi or the Tiwa of Taos. With the retreat of the Tiwa of Taos farther into their mountain retreat, Vargas ordered the storehouses of Taos broken into and the grain stored within loaded on mules for cargo to Santa Fe. With departure of the afternoon and the appearance in the night sky of mountain smoke, various members of the Vargas expedition suggested that a safer route north through the San Antonio Mountains, across Culebra Creek before descending in the direction of Costilla Creek, be set out upon for arrival in Santa Fe. On June 20, Vargas had the voice of the Town crier announce to the citizens of Santa Fe, the pending departure, with the intent to subdue the Tewa of Jémez and Keresan of Santo Domingo, of a select group of Santa Feans.

From the deserted Pueblo of Ciénguilla, Vargas and his forces traveled on the 21st of July to Santo Domingo Pueblo. Whilst en-camped in Santo Domingo Pueblo, Vargas received a plea for protection and men from Governor Bartolomé de Ojeda of Santa Ana Pueblo. Vargas sent an immediate order for Ojeda to organize, for deployment, Keresan members of the Pueblos of Santa Ana, Sia and San Felipe.

With the forces of Santa Ana, Sia and San Felipe, as well as the weather on his side, Vargas once having divided his forces by night, sent Eusabio de Vargas and his forces and his Indian auxiliaries around to the far side of the peñol. With appearance of first light, Vargas and his forces overran during brief intensive encounters, the peñol of Jémez, taking the lives of eighty-four members of the Towa of Jémez and Keresan of Santo Domingo and imprisoning three hundred and forty-six Towa and Keresan women and children.

Although it would take "the women of Jémez over seven days to bring over four hundred and twenty fanegas of maize" which the Towa of Jémez and Keresan of Santo Domingo had accumulated on Jémez peñol down into Jémez Pueblo (his Keresan soldiers brought down fifty-five fanegas for their own use) arrangements were made in Santa Fe for the Franciscan Farfán de Godos to provide carts for the transference of the maize in question from San Felipe to Santa Fe. 1

On his return to Santa Fe, capitán Antonio Jorgé encountered 2 members of Jémez Pueblo each of whom had been waiting, in front of San Felipe Pueblo, for the army of Santa

Fe. The natives of Jémez claimed to represent seventy-two men and women all of whom had escaped from the peñol of Jémez during the battle between the Spaniards, Towa of Pecos, Keresan of San Felipe, Santa Ana & Sia against the Towa of Jémez and the Tewa of Santo Domingo.

According to the representatives from Jémez Pueblo, the governor of Jémez who had suffered a broken leg during the battle for Jémez Pueblo, desired to offer a leader of the uprising of 1694 to Governor Vargas in exchange for safe conduct into Jémez Pueblo once again. Vargas accepted, with good grace the surrender of the governor of Jémez, whereas the Franciscans intervened on the behalf of the leader of the Jémez uprising, saving one life for future development in New Mexico.

In order to quicken the return of the Towa of Jémez to their pueblo, the Towa of Jémez would have to provide one half the male members of their pueblo to Vargas' quest to reduce the Tewa and Tano of San Ildefonso or Black Mesa. With the whole hearted agreement of the Towa of Jémez, Vargas drew up his plans for the conquest of the Tano & Tewa of Black Mesa.

Once having given the Towa of Jémez a cord with five day knots (the fifth day knot was to be undone on the day the Towa reached Santa Fe), Vargas had the town crier, Jusupe, announce on 1 September, 1694, the coming campaign for the siege of Black Mesa. With fifty soldiers, fifty militia-men and one hundred and fifty Puebloans from Pecos, San Felipe, Santa Ana, Sia and Jémez, Vargas set out for San Ildefonso or Black Mesa on September, 4th, 1694.

During an engagement of three to four hours with the Tano and Tewa of Black Mesa, nothing was accomplished. Eleven Spaniards who had been wounded during the battle for the msea in question, were sent to Santa Fe for medical treatment.

During the afternoon, the Spaniards and their Pueblo allies, with their backs to the river and their faces to the mesa made another unsuccessful effort during which 2 members of the Spaniards' forces lost their lives., to reach the top of San Ildefonso Mesa. Subsequently, the Tano and Tewa of San Ildefonso Mesa, having made efforts to prevent the Spaniards from loading the former's fall of harvest of maize from the river valley land near, finally offered to come down on their own in order to treat with de Vargas. Vargas, alone with his alfárez, went to the base of the peñol to receive the surrender of the Tano and Tewa of San Ildefonso Mesa. Once in Santa Fe, Vargas would write in his Journal:

> I called them my children and told them how it had grieved me the other time that
> I had come to learn that they had not made the resolve which they had made on
> this day. (I told them) that they should be very devout for this was the festival of our

Lady, and she had been in sorrow for them for she was our Mother and our Judge. I ordered the royal alfarez to show them our Lady of the Remedies whose image was on the royal banner. I assured them before the image of said divine lady, and by the Holy Cross of the Rosary, that in the name of his majesty, the king, I pardoned them all those were living on the mesa. All of the people were viewing this momentous scene. Lastly, I told them that I had buried beneath the soil all that they had done this day, and that form this day forword, they should always have to remember what they done on this day; which was to promise me that they would live again as Christians and be very devout subjects of his majesty.[55]

With the triumphant return of the Vargas expedition to Santa Fe, the Towa leaders of Jémez came to Santa Fe to remind Vargas of the promise he had made to the leaders of Jémez Pueblo before the siege of San Ildefenso or Black Mesa. Vargas graciously complied with the promise he had made to Jémez Pueblo, releasing from servitude in Santa Fe, the women and children of Jémez into the hands of the Jémez leaders.

The realization that Vargas had kept his word, fell like a pebble in pond across Northern New Mexico, exhibiting a ripple effect on the Tewa Pueblos of Tesuque, Nambé, Jacona, Cuyamungé, Santa Clara, San Juan and San Ildefenso; all of whose members were to return peacefully to their pueblos On September 17, 1694, Vargas set out, in the name of the Spanish King, Carlos II, on a re-possession tour of the Tewa Pueblos of Tesusque, Nambé, Cuyamungé, Santa Clara, San Juan and San Ildefenso, repeating in each pueblo "Long live Carlos II, rey de España and all his kingdom and its lands and its pueblos, and these native subjects his vassals."

With potential peaceful return of the Tewa to their pueblos, Vargas sought immediately to answer the question of how to provide the settlers of Santa Fe with sufficient provender or grain. Once having arranged for the sale and transference of three thousand fanegas of maize from the Parral Valley, Vargas wrote to el virrey el Conde de Galve in order to request payment for the grain in question. Luís Granillo, who had been left in charge of Paso del Norte, with the departure of Vargas' reconnaissance expedition of August 1692, was ordered to depart for Nueva Vizcaya in order to purchase another three thousand fanegas of grain. With over one hundred soldiers and their families, numerous Franciscans and innumerable members of a natural group known as "medio-ambiente" or half-group to provide for, Vargas, who could reach el virrey only though an intermediate person known as el royal fiscal,

---

[55]   Kessell, John. Kiva, Cross and Crown. Department of the Interior, Washington D. C. 1979.

impressed upon el virrey with the necessity for the Spaniards of Santa Fe to (a) refrain from further use of Pueblo Indian grain and (b) to become self sufficient.

Once having received, on the other hand, a petition from the Franciscans of New Mexico to return to their pueblos, Vargas and his escort left Santa Fe in order to install Diego Zeinos, as missionary for Pecos Pueblo. After the model of governance which had been previously introduced, under a governor, alcalde or justicia and alguacil or sheriff, to the Towa of Pecos during March of 1691, by the members of the Castaño de Sosa expedition, the Spaniard, Francisco de Anaya Almazán, was selected as alaclde or mayor of Pecos, whereas certain Towa of Pecos Indians were democratically elected (with a great deal of reason) to the positions of governor, lieutenant-governor, alcaldes, church-workers and captains of war, respectively. Juan de Alpuente was installed as missionary at Zia and of the visita or visiting station of Santa Ana.

With the settling of the Franciscans within their missions at Pecos, San Felipe, Sia, Jémez, Tesuque, Pojoaque, Jacona, Santa Clara, San Ildefenso, San Juan, San Cristóbal, Picuríes and Taos throughout 1695, and the gradual diminishment of the strength of the Spaniards of Santa Fe, the Pueblo Indians of New Mexico began to show signs of un-rest and dis-satisfaction with the Franciscans of New Mexico specifically and the Spaniards of New Mexico in general.

CHAPTER X

THE PUEBLO REVOLT OF **1696**

The Franciscan Corvera, who had ridden more miles and acquired more experience in New Mexico than any other religious person who was living in New Mexico at the time, recounted in 1696 to custos Francisco de Vargas how he, the former, had crept up to a San Ildefenso "estufa" or kiva (Pueblo Indian social, economic and religious meeting place) in order to listen in on a conversation, which was taking place between the Tewa Indians of San Ildefenso during the late night of December 20, 1695.

Corvera forbade, however, Francisco de Vargas to tell Governor Vargas of the nature of the conversation in question for the very same reason Governor Vargas would decide in time not to give countenance to the rumor of another Pueblo revolt. Neither Francisco de Corvera nor Diego de Vargas desired to cause the Pueblo Indians un-rest.

After having received word, however, from more than one source, of an impending revolt, custos Francisco de Vargas went directly to Governor Diego de Vargas with the news of the general state of un-rest among the pueblos of New Mexico. Various Franciscans, such as Navarro of Picuríes and Diez of Taos, traveled to Santa Fe in order to inform Governor Vargas of the plans of certain Pueblos to rise up. Governor Vargas thought, having sent thirty soldiers to guard Taos and another group beyond the River San Juan, that he had done as much as possible to safeguard the Franciscans of Santa Fe

At this point in the impending state and church crisis in Santa Fe, custos de Vargas took it upon himself to let the Franciscans tell him how many soldiers each mission would require in order to feel secure.

At Pecos, the Franciscan Fray Juan Alpuente requested the immediate presence of six well armed and "God-fearing" soldiers. The Franciscan Fray Antonio Cisneros of Cochití made no request for soldiers to be sent to protect his person. The Franciscan Fray Diego de Ramirez, resident missionary of San Felipe, had already departed, for reasons of health to Bernalillo. The Franciscan Fray Pedro de Matha of Sia requested six soldiers for the protection of his person. The Franciscan Frairs Miguel de Trizo and Jesús María Casañas of Jémez and San Diego de la Monte respectively; requested for protection six soldiers form Santa Fe.

The Franciscan Prieto, writing from San Juan, informed Vargas of the plans of the Tewa of San Juan to rise up. And finally, Domingo, one day to be known as Domingo Romero, informant, scout, and governor of Tesuque, wrote to describe a meeting which had taken place between certain Pueblo Indians from San Cristóbal [catalystic site for the uprising in question], San Lázaro, Santa Clara, Nambé, Jacona, Cuyamungé and Tesuque with the express intent of forming another pueblo revolt. Due to the exposed position of the mission of Tesuque, he would leave the number of men required for its protection up to Governor Vargas.

According to the second petition, which custos Francisco de Vargas had made to Governor Diego de Vargas, the missionaries of Taos, Picuríes, Santa Clara, San Juan, San Cristóbal, Pecos, Sia, San Juan de Jémez and San Diego de Jémez, would require sixty soldiers in order to feel secure. For the benefit of the Franciscan de Vargas, Governor Vargas calculated immediately the number of soldiers he would require in order to insure the safety of Santa Fe. Ten soldiers had always been necessary to guard the towers of Santa Fe. The governor had to have sixty soldiers in order to guard, within two separate contingents, the horses of Santa Fe. And twenty-four soldiers had been sent to accompany the departure of the Santa Fe-Paso del Norte commissary carts. Thus, Vargas was left with four soldiers; ready for distribution among the Pueblos of New Mexico. Well aware of Vargas' position in Santa Fe, the Franciscans of New Mexico took it upon themselves to seek refuge in Santa Fe, Santa Cruz and Bernallilo.

Governor Vargas was unable to comprehend, however, that the Pueblos of New Mexico had chosen to act upon the real as well as the un-real (in their minds) weaknesses of the Spaniards; rather than any decision, such as the removal of livestock from Santa Clara Pueblo, he might make.

At this point in time, Vargas had the will to believe in the Pueblo Indians of New Mexico, whereas the Franciscans of New Mexico—Juan Alpuente of Pecos, Diego Zeinos of Tesuque, Antonio Moreno of Nambé, Alonso Jimeniz de Cisneros of Cochití, Francisco Covera of San Ildefenso, Blas Navarro of San Juan, José Arzibu of San Cristóbal, Antonio Carbonel of Taos, Miguel de Trizo of Jémez and Fray Francisco de Jesús of San Diego de al Monte—had the will and resolve to act, in as much as such persons were able to inform custos Francisco de Vargas of the state of the Pueblo Indians of New Mexico.

In order to ease his doubts as to the real state of the Pueblo Indians of New Mexico, Vargas wrote to el virrey, el Conde de Galve in Mexico City, stating that Santa Fe was and would be in great danger until el virrey could send five hundred families and one hundred soldiers to New Mexico. Vargas also requested 'one thousand five hundred cattle per year and clothing for wives, widows, children, orphans from the families brought up from Sombrerete and Zacatecas. With knowledge of the fact that Vargas could do little to insure their safety within the Pueblos of New Mexico, the Franciscans of New Mexico took it upon themselves to return, as they had taken upon themselves to leave, the Pueblos of New Mexico.

Intelligence on Pueblo Revolt of 1696 seeped into Santa Fe throughout the day of Monday, June 4th. The Franciscan Cisneros of Cohcití sent a Pueblo runner to Santa Fe with the news of the decision of Keresan of Cochití to depart in the direction of Cochití Mesa. Cisneros, himself, had departed in the direction of the Keresan Pueblo of San Felipe, where he was able to encounter Capitan Fernando de Chávez and a small group of settlers. From Tesuque, Governor Domingo sent word to Vargas of the actual rise of the Tiwa of Picuríes and Taos, the Keresan of Santo Domingo and Cochití and Tano of San Cristóbal and San Lázaro.

On June 5th without knowledge of either the causes of the Pueblo Revolt of 1696 or the physical direction the pueblo revolt had taken, Vargas was able, nonetheless, to send powder and balls to Roque de la Madrid, who had been able to reach Santa Cruz de la Cañada; request the presence of Governor Felipe Chisto of Pecos and his auxiliaries in Santa Fe; and order the mayor or alcalde of Bernallilo, Fernando de Chávez to collect Spaniards from Cochití and Bernallilo as well as Keresan from Santa and San Felipe for craft construction and consequently, river crossings of the Rio Grande in flood.

Of the three figures in question, only Fernando de Chávez, who had been unable to convince the Keresan of Sia, Santa Ana, and San Felipe, to collect their agricultural surplus for river crossings of el Río Grande, would be unable to adhere to the orders of Governor Vargas.[56]

From Santa Cruz de la Cañada, alcalde mayor of San Juan, Roque de la Madrid and his small group of soldiers reconnoitered in the direction of San Cristóbal only to discover the no longer living remains of José Arzibu of San Cristóbal and Antonio Carbonel of Taos.

---

[56]   Espinosa, J. Manuel. The Pueblo Indian Revolt of 1696. {Norman, Oklahoma. University of Oklahoma Press. 1988.} page 267

At Ohkay Owingeh Pueblo, the Spaniard, Juan de Archuleta, had been able to free the soldier Mateo Lovato and the Franciscan, Blas Navarro from the convent of San Juan. Having reached San Ildefonso Pueblo, de la Madrid discovered the remains of Juana de Almazán and members of her family. The Franciscans Francisco Corvera and Antonio Moreno of Nambé, having enclosed themselves within el convento de San Ildefonso, had smothered to death therein due to the firing of it by certain members of the Tewa in question.

Governor Bartolome de Ojeda, who had written form Santa Ana Pueblo in order to request powder and ball, had been able to recognize, with the discovery of and consequently, communication forthwith to Santa Fe, the first natural appearance of the Pueblo Revolt of 1696; in the form of human and horse tracks leading from Jémez Pueblo in the direction of Acoma Pueblo to the near northeast.

On the morning of June 11, 1696, 2 leaders of the Pueblo Revolt of 1696,

Luis Cuniju of Jémez and Diego Xenome, a cacique from Nambé, had arrived at the entry to Pecos Pueblo. Each man had come to Pecos with the idea to enlist support from the rebel faction within Pecos for the on-going pueblo revolt.

Governor Felipe of Pecos was quick to dispel any notion Cuniju and Zenome may have had concerning the enlistment of Pecos Pueblo on the side of the rebel pueblos by saying: "Here we are loyal to the king." Diego, a leader of the rebel faction at Pecos, was taken out and strung up on a local tree, whereas Xenome and Cuniju were taken to Santa Fe, where they would be questioned as to the origin of the Pueblo Revolt of 1696 before being taken out and shot in front of the Church of San Miguel. Whether Cuniju or Xenome would have gone to Pecos Pueblo had they known of Governor Felipe's friendship with Governor Vargas, remains open to historical conjecture.

Given Pecos had been divided, at least since the arrival of Castaño de Sosa expedition of July 1590, between 2 political factions.

On June 11, 1696, Vargas received word from Governor Domingo of an impending assault on Tesuque Pueblo by the mulatto, Domingo Naranjo, and puebloans from Santa Clara and San Ildefonso Once having transferred a small group of Santa Feans to Tesuque by night, Vargas would have to be satisfied with the faint heartedness of El Naranjo by day. For his entry into the mountains of Chimayo, Vargas chose to make Santa Cruz de la Cañada, which was located centrally among the risen pueblos of New Mexico, his temporary headquarters.

With full knowledge of the fact that most members of the arisen pueblos would have to return to their pueblos, Vargas and his Santa Fean, Pecos and Tesuque forces set out from

Santa Cruz de la Cañada in the direction of the mountains to the north at 9:00 p. m. on the evening of July 1st 1696. Having arrived at 2:00 a. m. in the morning of the next day, Vargas and his forces waited until dawn before moving on and dispersing the Tiwa of Picuríes numerous of whom had set up camp on the river that runs south from their pueblo.

Upon his return to Santa Cruz de la Cañada, Vargas received promising news from capitán Miguel de Lara whose force, although ambushed on the way to and upon departing from San Diego Mesa, had been able to retrieve the body of the Franciscan Jesus María Casañas.

By July 10, 1696, Vargas and his small group of Santa Feans, forty-five members of Pecos Pueblo, eleven members of Tesuque and governors of San Felipe, Santa Ana and Sia had met on the eastern bank of the Rio Grande near San Felipe Pueblo in order to draw up plans for search and disperse actions against members of Cochití and Santo Domingo Pueblos, the majority of whom had taken refuge within the mountains near Cochití Pueblo. Upon encountering the temporary encampment of Pueblos in question, Vargas and his force routed a group of Pueblo families before picking up thirty-one women and children as well as one hundred fanegas of maize for the under-fed settlers of Santa Fe.

To the southeast, the Tiwa of Picuríes and the Tiwa of Taos had been seen assembling in a canyon near Pecos. The native sightings caused the Spaniards of Santa Fe to momentarily contract. With the decision of the Puebloans in question not to move against the Spaniards of Santa Fe, Vargas deployed under Antonio Valverde and Governor Domingo of Tesuque, south from Santa Cruz de la Cañada in order to root the Tewa of Nambé and Cuyamungé out of the mountains on the other side of Nambé Pueblo. Once having returned to Santa Cruz de la Cañada, Vargas and his force drew up plans to confront El Naranjo and his forces from Santo Domingo.

Upon his arrival in front of el Embudo Canyon, which is located to the northeast of Ohkay Owingeh, Capitán Lázaro Mizquía and a handful of Spaniards was to penetrate into the Canyon in question in order to defy the Keresan of Santo Domingo numerous of whom had taken up positions along its sides. With the arrival of auxiliarios, the Spaniards and Puebloans who had entered Embudo Canyon were able, after having taken the life El Naranjo, to battle their way out of the canyon in question. From Sia Pueblo, Vargas set out with a small groups of Spaniards and auxiliarios from Pecos, Santa Fe, Santa Ana, and Sia for Acoma Pueblo, where very few Keresan from Cochití and Towa from Jémez had taken up refuge for a time. Without the manpower to overcome Acoma Peñol, Vargas decided to level (within an act which would remain without historical resonance)the agricultural fields at the base of Acoma Pueblo before returning to Santa Fe.

Upon his return to Santa Fe, Vargas learned of the surrender of 2 leaders of the Pueblo Revolt of 1696: Miguel Saxsette and Juan Griego, war captain from Picuríes Pueblo. Vargas immediately sent the latter surrender terms, which were unfortunately ignored, to the future woe of the Tiwa of Picuríes numerous of whose leaders would be enslaved for a time among the Cuartelejo Apache of future southwestern Kansas before being liberated by the Spaniards of Santa Fe during the early 1700's.

With once again only the Tiwa of Taos and Tiwa of Picuríes to convince and convert, Vargas must have had the same feeling of elation which had had felt in 1694, when he had the will to believe in his capacity to rule the Spaniards and the Pueblos of New Mexico

Having discovered Picuríes Pueblo deserted in anticipation of the arrival of the Spaniards of Santa Fe, Vargas and his forces rode northeast in the direction of Taos Pueblo. Upon his arrival near Taos Pueblo, which the Tiwa of Taos had left for their mountain retreat, Vargas pleaded, upon encountering the Tiwa of Taos in the mountains, with the taseños to return to their Pueblo. With the refusal of the Tiwa of Taos to come down out of the mountains, Vargas divided their forces into three groups for entry into the Taos mountain retreat. Having left Luís Granillo and Antonio Valverde at the entrance to the canyon in question, Vargas deployed, with a small group on the upper reaches of the mountain valley to the right, whereas Roque de la Madrid deployed with a small group on the mountain valley to the left.

With the simultaneous descent of Vargas' and Madrids' forces, the Tiwa of Taos abandoned their food supply, and their deer and elk skin robes to the Spaniards and pueblo members of Pecos, San Felipe, Santa Ana, and Sia. With fall of heavy snow on Taos Pueblo the next day, the Tiwa of Taos decided, under verbal pressure from Vargas to return to Taos Pueblo. Once again, Vargas served as town greeter to the Tiwa who would be returning to their pueblo.

With the Triumph of his forces over the Tiwa of Taos, Vargas just did not ride off into the Sunset of relations with el virrey el Conde de Galve. Vargas suggested, instead, that the Tiwa of Taos come often to Santa Fe in order to inform him of the state of being within their pueblo.

If the report of la Junta de Hacienda had stated (without knowledge of the outcome of the Pueblo Revolt of 1694) within a letter to Santa Fe in early 1694, that the aid Vargas would soon be receiving would be the last he could hope for, the very same Junta de Hacienda, would state in September of 1696, (with full knowledge of the results of the Pueblo Revolt of 1696) that sufficient aid would be forthcoming for the permanent foundation of Santa Fe.

CHAPTER XI

THE DIEGO DE VARGAS AND PEDRO RODRÍQUEZ CUBERO IMBROGLIO EN SANTA FE

Diego de Vargas, who had been appointed to the governorship of New Mexico on June 18, 1688, and would come to the governorship of New Mexico on February 22, 1691, petitioned in May of 1693 (after the appointment of Pedro Rodríquez y Cubero to the governorship of New Mexico on June 24, 1692), the Spanish King Carlos II, for consideration of an appointment either to the post of governor and capitán-general of Guatemala or other posts within the Spanish Empire. Vargas, who would soon be, according to his contract, out of work, was completely justified in making such a request.

As the time of his governorship wound down, Vargas, who had remained without a response to his request, petitioned for permission to remain in New Mexico for another gubernatorial term. In the interim, Vargas worked, through his Mexico City lawyer, Goncalez-Calderon, in order to impress el virrey Moctezuma with the fact that New Mexico was (a) nothing more (in the aftermath of the Pueblo Revolt of 1680)than Paso del Norte or El Paso and (b) New Mexico would be in great danger if Cubero came to the governorship in question.

Vargas was making, at this point in time, an effort to convince el virrey Moctezuma that his (the former's) presence in New Mexico was, as it had been, indispensable.

When Pedro Rodríquez Cubero rode into Santa Fe on July 2nd 1697, Diego de Vargas was not disposed to give up the governorship of New Mexico. Vargas had remained (there having been no other authority figure for hundreds of miles) one year and just over four months beyond the five year (1691-96) limit of his contract. Upon arrival in Santa Fe, Cubero was to carry out a residencia into the governorship of Diego de Vargas. Cubero, at the request of the cabildo of Santa Fe, however, extended his residencia (unaware, perhaps, that this was against Spanish law) of Vargas (even though nothing had been brought to light against Vargas) beyond the one month limit prescribed by Spanish law.

The majority of Santa Fe citizens accused the former governor of playing favorites; embezzling large amounts of money that had been turned over to him by the Royal Treasury for the development of the colony; taking the lives of eighty-four defenders of Santa Fe (thereby contributing to the Pueblo uprisings of 1694; releasing from servitude among the settlers of Santa Fe numerous Pueblo Indians; preventing the Spaniards of Santa Fe and Nueva Vizcaya from conducting business between Santa Fe and Nueva Vizcaya ; of poorly distributing the food supplies of Santa Fe and ruling Santa Fe without the counsel of the city council of Santa Fe. Vargas had, of course, ruled Santa Fe with aid of his "servants" and leading soldiers Juan Páez Hurtado and Antonio Valverde.[57]

Vargas, having been found guilty, by Cubero, of the charges which had been brought against the former governor by three hundred settlers of Santa Fe, was fined four thousand pesos and placed under house arrest on October 2, 1697. Future governor of New Mexico, Antonio Valverde, was supposedly exiled (according to Cubero) from New Mexico on October 14, 1697, [he would leave New Mexico, on his own, for medical motives prior to October 14, 1697], whereas future interim governor of New Mexico, Juan Páez Hurtado, was arrested on October 29, 1697.

In order to re-enforce his desire to remain in New Mexico and impress the Spanish King Carlos II, Vargas petitioned through his lawyer, Goncalez-Calderon in November of 1695, for permission within a "memorial" or brief to acquire, after the conclusion of Cubero's term, the governorship of New Mexico once again; the honorific of marqués; plus an un-specified encomienda grant (en lieu of a pension from the Spanish government) of 6,000 pesos.[58]

On February 4, 1697, the council of the Indies or Consejo de los Indias, the most reasonable Spanish governing body of the era and the most powerful ruling body within the Spanish Empire after the Spanish king, approved his Memorial, after having considered the reservations shown by the royal fiscal over Vargas' request for an encomienda grant of 4000 pesos.[59]

---

[57] Accusation of the Cabildo of Santa Fe., 1697. S. F. S. cited in Twitchell, Ralph. Spanish Archives 11 pages 112-14.

[58] Consul Record, A. G. I. Guadalajara 141

[59] Ibid.

Guarding his reservation over the advisability of affirming Vargas' request for an encomienda grant among the Pueblo Indians all of whom had been liberated from the necessity, requirements and evolution of la encomienda, Carlos II confirmed the recommendations of the Council of the Indies, referring to the success of and development in New Mexico as 'due (with aid of divine intervention) to the valor, zeal and dis-interestedness of Diego de Vargas.[60]

At this point in time, Vargas' strengths could be discovered among the members of his family; various of whom had taken up residence at the royal court; within the voice of the former custos of New Mexico, Francisco de Vargas; and according to his friend and relative, Nicólas Ortíz. With the third petition of Vargas for an encomienda grant and due to the arrival in the hands of Carlos II of Vargas written record of the Pueblo Revolt of 1696, the Spanish king capitulated, granting within a cédula réal from the Council of the Indies, on August 24, 1698, Vargas, an encomienda grant of four thousand pesos. The son of Diego de Vargas, Juan Manuel, would receive (for application in New Mexico only what would be, for all intents and purposes) the last formal encomienda grant (he would not activate it) to have been granted in New Mexico.[61]

With arrival in New Mexico of the news of the re-appointment (due in part to the recommendation of el virrey Moctezuma (1696-1701) of Diego de Vargas to the governorship of New Mexico on February 21, 1699, and the appointment of Antonio Valverde to the position of captaincy-general of Paso del Norte, Governor Cubero and the Santa Fe 300 wrote four letters of denunciation to el virrey Moctezuma, pleading with him to renounce the re-appointment of Diego de Vargas to the governorship of New Mexico and Antonio Valverde to the captaincy-general of Paso del Norte; Paso del Norte having been, the principal entryway and supply station for Santa Fe.

Given the denunciations of Governor Cubero and the settlers of Santa Fe would have to pass through the hands of el fiscal réal; a man whose limitations had weighed decisively against Vargas' repeated request for men and material during his governorship.

Because Antonio Valverde had collected recommendations of service from Diego de Vargas, and even Pedro Rodríquez Cubero, it is difficult to imagine that the former, Valverde, would have compromised himself during the time Pedro Rodríquez Cubero was recognized as the governor of New Mexico. Cubero, who was only able to think of bringing charge of sedition against Vargas, implored el virrey Moctezuma not to let Vargas come to the

---

[60] Ibid.
[61] A. G. I. Guadalajara 141 1643-46 102-106

governorship of New Mexico; after the departure of the governor from the governorship of New Mexico; a stipulation which had already been met in Vargas' new contract.

Between November 18, 1699 and April 3,1700, Cubero called for twenty-six Santa Feans to testify to the following charges :" (1) Vargas had been stirring up trouble since December of 1697 by spreading news that he had been re-appointed to the governorship of New Mexico; news that he awaited daily; (2) he was offering favors to those who would take his side in the coming litigation'(3) he was attempting to cover up debts and fraudulent uses of the royal funds by bribery; (4) he was threatening those who had testified against him.[62]

In response to the testimony of the Santa Fe twenty-six, Cubero confined Vargas, once again, to his house where he was "maintained incommunicado" or without communication, with access only to members of his family and Catholic Mass. Because Vargas had refused to recognize the charges which Cubero and the Santa Fe and the Santa Fe twenty-six had brought against the former governor of New Mexico, he was placed in irons within his house on March 8, 1700.

If Cubero had brought charges against Vargas the moment the new governor entered Santa Fe, he may have been in a position to justify his actions. For Vargas was, at that moment, no longer the governor of New Mexico. Cubero waited until Vargas had been re-appointed to the governorship of New Mexico before bringing charges against the former and future governor of New Mexico. Cubero had pronounced Vargas of being guilty of defying a royal order, when he was no longer guilty of such an act.

With presentation across the months of November and December of 1699 of the final pleas for consideration of their respective clients, Juan Saluda, who represented Cubero and the Santa Fe three hundred and José de Ledesma, who represented Diego de Vargas and Antonio Valverde, to the royal authorities in Mexico City, the argument of pleyto which had risen between Diego de Vargas and Antonio Valverde on the one hand and Pedro Rodríquez Cubero on the other, was on its way to resolution.[63]

Juan Saluda had been designated as the captain-general of Paso del Norte by Governor Cubero in July 1697. When Antonio Valverde arrived in Mexico City, with his designation as captain-general of Paso del Norte, that was how the question of governmental succession in Paso del Norte stood.

According to Saluda, Valverde, as a servant of Vargas would(1) be a dangerous element in Paso del Norte; (2) between Santa Fe and Paso del Norte there would be no cooperation;

---

[62] Autos hechos criminals contra el general Diego de Vargas. A. G. N. Santa Fe Vinculos tomo 14
[63] Nuevo Mexico. Año de 1699. En Nueve Cuadernos

(3)Valverde lacked the ten years experience necessary to rule Paso del Norte; (4) Valverde had committed acts of fraud against the Spanish Treasury; (5) Valverde was responsible for the deaths of four Spanish missionaries during the Pueblo Revolt of 1696; (6) the charges brought against Valverde in Santa Fe indicated that he was not competent to rule Paso del Norte;(7) Valverde was not disposed to distribute salaries to the soldiers of Paso del Norte; (8) the matter was of concern to Cubero who had 90,000 pesos invested in the affairs of New Mexico; (9) that if Valverde was appointed to the captaincy-general of Paso del Norte he would respond with rancor and vengeance' The fact remains that the majority of the charges brought by Cubero against Valverde were based on presumption.

The first decision of the royal fiscal, which came down on the side of Diego de Vargas, stated that Governor Cubero's conduct of the residency of Diego de Vargas, which went beyond the thirty day prescribed according to Spanish law, was against the procedure of Spanish law; and referring to the fact, in his opinion, that the charges which had been brought in secret and with the compliance of certain Santa Fe citizens were without foundation. The charge of "fraud against the royal treasury" was to be resolved by a member of the Spanish Treasury of Durango.

With the full and complete consideration for the recommendations which Antonio Valverde had solicited and collected from Diego de Vargas, Francisco de Vargas and Pedro Rodríquez Cubero and respect for the decision of the Spanish king to appoint Valverde to the captaincy-general of Paso del Norte, the royal fiscal exonerated Valverde of all charges which had been brought against him and affirmed his appointment to the captaincy-general of Paso del Norte. The Royal Council or junta real with one ear on the ground in Santa Fe and the other attuned to Spanish law, ordered Cubero to send Vargas' monetary records to Mexico City, without delay, (the Royal Treasury came, after examining Vargas' monetary records, to the conclusion, that it owed him 17, 619 pesos and 2 tomines 6 granos.[64]) with charges to be brought if he failed to comply.[65]

[64]   Kessell, John. A Settling of Accounts. (Alburquerque, New Mexico. UNM Press. 2002). Page 83
[65]   Report of the Royal Fiscal. Mexico City. 1700

BIBLIOGRAPHY

1. Barrett, Elinore M. Conquest and Catastrophe. Alburquerque, New Mexico. UNM Press. 2002.
2. Benavides, Alonso de. Memorial. Madrid, España. 1630.
3. Bloom, Lansing. The New Mexico Historical Review. July, 1930.
4. Burkholder, Marc. Johnson, Lyman. Colonial Latin American. Oxford Press, London, England. 1988.
5. Chávez, Fray Angélico. The Origins of Spanish Families in New Mexico. Museum of New Mexico Press.
6. Dozier, Edward. The Pueblo Indians of North America. Waveland Press, Prospect Heights, Illinois. 1942.
7. Espinosa, J. Crusaders of the Rio Grande. Institute of Jesuit Studies. Chicago, Illinois. 1942.
8. Hackett, Charles Wilson (editor) and Charmion Clair Shelby (translator). Revolt of the Pueblo Indians of New Mexico and Otermín's Attempted Reconquest, 1680-1682. (Albuquerque: The University of New Mexico Press, 1942). Volume 9, pages 232-253.
9. Hallenbeck, Cleve. Land of the Conquistadores. Caxton Press. Caldwell, Idaho. 1950.
10. Jones, O. Pueblo Warriors. The University of Oklahoma Press. 1966.
11. Kessell, John. Kiva, Cross and Crown. Department of the Interior, Washington D. C. 1979.
12. Linder, Peter. Latin American Studies. Highlands University. Las Vegas, New Mexico. 1992.
13. Scholes, France V. The New Mexico Historical Review. 1932.
14. Simmons, Marc. The Last Conquistador. University of Oklahoma Press. Norman, Oklahoma. 1991.
15. Stanley, Francis. (Luís). Ciudad Santa Fe. The World Press. Denver, Colorado. 1958.
16. Twitchell, Ralph. Antigua Santa Fe. The University of New Mexico Press. 1997.
17. Weber, Chris. The Myth of Santa Fe. The University of New Mexico Press. 1997.
18. Weber, David,. The Spanish Northern Frontier. Yale University. New Haven, Connect. 1998.

Index of Names

NOTES ON IMPORTANT PERSONAGES

A

Acevedo, Gaspar Zuniga. The Count of Monterrey: first virrey to question and to largely unsuccessfully alter Juan de Oñate's contract or recapitulaciones for the settlement of New Mexico (1598-1607).

Acoma Pueblo: Keresan Pueblo whose members were active during the Pueblo Revolt of 1680 if not during the Pueblo of 1696.

Adelantado: title or honorific, among Spaniards, signifying first person of royal entry or "lord of the march;" given to the first and last adelantado to New Mexico, Governor Juan de Oñate at the insistence of his brother, Alonso de Oñate, at the Spanish Royal Court in 1601.

Ágreda, María Jesús: Abess of the Convento de la Purisima Concepción; confident and friend of Philip IV.

Ayeta, Francisco: Franciscan director of the Santa Fe Commissary carts (1664+1681)); receptor or the news of the Pueblo Revolt of 1680 at Paso del Norte river crossing.

B

Benavides, Alonso de: custos or custodian, comisario or commissary and primer agente de la Inquisición Mexicana en Nuevo Méjico.

Black Mesa or San Ildefenso Mesa: principle site of the Tewa and Tano defense after the Spaniards' re-conquest and re-settlement of Santa Fe.

C

Caderyeta, marqués de: virrey of Nueva España and person most responsible for the appointment of Luís Rosas to the governor—ship of New Mexico (1637-41)

Catatí, Alonso: mestizo leader of the Pueblo Revolt of 1680 and leader of the resistance to the Spaniards' proposed re-settlement of New Mexico in 1681-82.

Ceballos, Bernardino: third governor of New Mexico; first governor to openly break after the reign of Pedro de Peralta, with the Franciscans of New Mexico.

Cerrillos: ancient pre-historic mining site of the Pueblo Indians; explored and mined for lead, silver, and turquoise by members of the Castaño de Sosa expedition; and independently by the members of the Juan de Oñate expedition to New Mexico; re-established, as a settlement site, by Governor Diego de Vargas after 1694.

Chavarría, Miguel de : 17; Custodian or custos of New Mexico (1620/21 1622)

Cochití Pueblo: one of the first New Mexico Indian Pueblos to have revolted against the Spaniards during 1694 and 1696.

Cordova, Diego de. el marqués de Guadalcázar: independent virrey of Nueva España (1614-21); responsible for bringing former governor Juan de Oñate to trial in Mexico City in 1614; advocate for the Royal Order of 1620.

Coronado, Francisco Vázquez de: explorer and leader, under el virrey Antonio de Mendoza, of the second Spanish exploratory expedition to the New Land to the North (`1540-43)inspiration for the passage of the Colonization of Laws of 1573 for the Ordinances of his Majesty for the New Discoveries, Conquest and Pacification, under Philip II.

Cuartelejo Apache: Apache settlement which was located, conjecturally, in southeastern Kansas, site of the enslavement for a time of various members of the Tiwa of Picuríes

Cuyamungé: Tewa Pueblo of northeastern central New Mexico.

D

De Vargas, Diego: 28th or 29th governor of New Mexico.

De Vargas, Francisco: custos of New Mexico during the reign of Governor Diego de Vargas; person most responsible for the release of former governor Vargas from house arrest in Santa Fe.

Duran Andrés: Fraile Franciscan who lost, under questionable circumstances, his life at San Ildefenso Pueblo in 1675.

E

Eulate, Juan de: fourth governor of New Mexico; introduced the profit principle into the reason for being of New Mexico governors of the 1600's.

Escalante, Sylvestre y Velez: Franciscan promoter of Governor Barrolomé de Ojeda of Santa Ana Pueblo; explorer and notable historian of the late 1600's in Santa Fe.

F

Factionalism: at least 2 political factions had been active at Pecos Pueblo prior to the entry of the Castaño de Sosa expedition of 1590-91; at least 2 political factions at Acoma Pueblo prior to the entry, into it, of members of the Juan de Oñate expedition of 1598.

Franciscan religious order: Franciscan minor if not mendicant religious order which came into existence-begin under Francis Bernadone in Assisi, Italy in 1209, with the compliance of the great Pope Innocent III and, subsequently, Pope Honorious.

G

Galve, Conde de: virrey of Nueva España; sponsor, to various degrees, and admirer of Governor Diego de Vargas.

I

Indies, Council of the or Consejo de los Indias: Spanish ruling and administrative body second only to the Spanish king; formed in order to promote Spanish law in the New World; to regulate trade and oversee immigration to and from the New World at the great inland port of Seville and, late, Cadiz' contains in Seville, the A. G. I or Los Archivos Generales de los Indias.

Isabel reina: the persons most responsible at the Spanish Court for the discovery of the New World; sponsor of Cristóbal Colón or Christopher Columbus.

J

Jacona: Tewa Pueblo of northern New Mexico.

Javier, Francisco: intolerant secretary of Governor Francisco Treviño (1675-77); one of the Spaniards responsible for the Pueblo Revolt of 1680.

Jémez Pueblo: Towa language speaking pueblo of northern central New Mexico.

Jusupe: Santa Fe town crier during the Luís Rosas imbroglio in Santa Fe.

Jorgé, Antonio: valiant sergeant under the command of Governor Diego de Vargas.

Juárez, Andrés: Franciscan guardian of Pecos Pueblo between 1631-44.

Justa de Hacienda: ruling body in Mexico with the jurisdiction over the settlement of the Spanish frontier.

K

Kewa Pueblo or Santo Domingo: Tewa Pueblo of importance to the Spaniards' entry into New Mexico; active in the Pueblo Revolts of 1680 and 1696.

M

Martínez y Montoya, Juan: captain, secretary of the cabildo of San Gabriel, alcalde mayor or chief magistrate of San Gabriel;' founder (conjecturally between 1607 and 1610) during the reign of Juan de Oñate and before the reign of Pedro de Peralta of the plaza of Santa Fe.

Manso, Juan: governor of New Mexico (1656-59); arrested after the residencia conducted by Governor López de Mendízabal; returned as alguacil or sheriff of Santa Fe with the Franciscan Alonso de Posada in 1661; arrested Lopez de Mendízabal; commissary of the Santa Fe commissary carts between 1764 and 1774.

Manso, Tómas: impeccable procurator-general of the Santa Fe commissary carts 1631-54.

Mendízabal, Bernardo López de: first Spanish governor to arrange wage rates for the Pueblo Indians of New Mexico.

N

Nambé Peublo: Tewa pueblo of northern central New Mexico

Navajo Nation: described by custos Alonso de Benavides as great agriculturalists.

O

Ojeda, Bartolomé de: among the first Pueblo Indians to return to New Mexico under the rule of Governor Diego de Vargas; governor of Santa Ana Pueblo; friend of and soldier for Governor Diego de Vargas.

Ohkay Owingeh or San Juan Pueblo:Tewa pueblo of northern central New Mexico; sympathetic to the cause of the Spaniards.

Oñate Juan de: first governor of New Mexico.

Ordöñez, Isidro: second commissary general of New Mexico and first supposed agent of the Mexican Inquisition.

Otermín, Antonio: twenty-fourth governor of New Mexico

P

Pacheco, Francisco: Tiwa leader of Taos Pueblo during the 1690's

Pacheco y Heredía, Francisco: eleventh governor of New Mexico. Pacheco-Osorio, Rodrigo de: el marqués de Cerralvo; virrey of Nueva España during the early 1620's.

Palace of the Governors: home and ruling site of the governors of New Mexico.

Pecos Pueblo: first pueblo of New Mexico to have been subjected, under Castaño de Sosa, to the Spanish conquest principle (December 31st, 1589-January 1st, 1590; site of the first Franciscan church to have been constructed in New Mexico; site for the distribution of trade goods among the Pueblos, Spaniards, Apache and Comanche.

Peinado, Fray Alonso de: 3; fourth Franciscan commissary of provisions for New Mexico after Fray Alonso Martínez, Juan de Escalona and Francisco Escobar.

Penetecost, Feast of: 10; to celebrate the descent of the Holy Spirit to the twelve disciples of Jesus.

Philip II(1556-98) Spanish king most responsible for the settlement of New Mexico; issued with New Mexico in mind in 1573, the Ordinances of his Majesty for the new discoveries, conquests and pacification; decreed the Ordenanza Patronato in 1754 which required the Franciscans of Nueva España or Mexico to travel to the near and far frontiers of the Spanish Empire in order to continue with their efforts to convert the natives of the New World to Catholicism.

Philip III Spanish king (1598-1621)13; encouraged the Count of Monterrey to provide aid for the members of the Oñate expedition in New Mexico; promoted the funding of the Franciscans in 1608; issued Royal Order of 1620 in order to make an effort to reconcile relations between the governors and the Franciscans of New Mexico.

Pueblo Indians of New Mexico whose members belong to the one or more of the original nine language families of New Mexico: Piro, Tompiro,

Keresan, Towa, Tewa, Tano, Southern Tiwa Northern Tiwa and Zuni.

R

Ramirez, Juan: 1656-64: custos and commissary of New Mexico who developed apart, in New Mexico, from the reign of Governor Bernardo López de Mendízabal

Requerimiento de 1512: first principle Spanish settlement law for the New World of the 1500's.

Repartimiento: Spanish institution for the acquisition of Indian labor.

Romero, Domingo: scout, Governor of Tesuque; leader of the Northern Pueblos and confidant of Governor Diego de Vargas.

Rosas, Luís: ninth governor of New Mexico.

S

Santa Fe: established un-officially between 1607-10 and officially in 1610

Santa Fe trade: first established un-officially, according to the entries of governors Luís Rosas and Bernardo López de Mendízabal.

Silva-Nieto, Francisco: sixth governor of New Mexico and second governor of New Mexico to cooperate with the Franciscans.

Socorro: The first New Mexico pueblo, after San Juan, to be named by Governor Juan de Oñate.

Sotelo-Osorio, Felipe: (1625-29); fifth governor of New Mexico

T

Taos Pueblo: Northern Tiwa Pueblo; active in the Pueblo Revolts of 1630, 1680, 1694 and 1696.

Tesuque Pueblo: northern central Pueblo; active in the Pueblo Revolts of 1680, 1694, and 1696; provided, under Domingo Romero, Governor Diego de Vargas with aid.

Treviño, Francisco: 47; governor of New Mexico most responsible for the Pueblo Revolt of 1680.

Tupatú, Luis; leader of the Pueblo Revolt of 1680; ally of Governor Diego de Vargas during his entry into New Mexico in September of 1693; co-refounder of Taos in 1692.

Tupatú, Lorenzo: brother of Luis Tupatú; captive of the Cuartelejo Apache after the Pueblo Revolt of 1696.

V

Velasco II, Luís: virrey of Nueva España (1590-1595) (1607-11)

Y

Yi, Juan: governor of Pecos Pueblo; allay of and provider for Governor Diego de Vargas' entries into Santa Fe; prevented massacre of the Diego de Vargas reconnaissance expedition near the intersection of the rivers Jémez and Río Grande.